600/-

A GIFT FOR:

_____

FROM:

_____

POTENTIAL
FOR EVERY DAY

OTHER BOOKS BY THE AUTHOR

AVAILABLE FROM DESTINY IMAGE PUBLISHERS

POTENTIAL
FOR EVERY DAY

Myles Munroe

Compiled by Angela Rickabaugh Shears.

DESTINY IMAGE® PUBLISHERS, INC.

P.O. Box 310, Shippensburg, PA 17257-0310

"Speaking to the Purposes of God for This Generation and for the Generations to Come."

This book and all other Destiny Image, Revival Press, Mercy Place, Fresh Bread, Destiny Image Fiction, and Treasure House books are available at Christian bookstores and distributors worldwide.

For a U.S. bookstore nearest you, call **1-800-722-6774**.

For more information on foreign distributors, call **717-532-3040**.

Or reach us on the Internet: www.destinyimage.com.

ISBN 10: 0-7684-2669-3
ISBN 13: 978-0-7684-2669-4

For Worldwide Distribution, Printed in the U.S.A.

2 3 4 5 6 7 8 9 10 11 / 12 11 10 09 08

Now to Him who is able to do immeasurably more than all we ask or imagine, according to His power that is at work within us (Ephesians 3:20).

The wealthiest spot on this planet is not the oil fields of Kuwait, Iraq, or Saudi Arabia. Neither is it the gold and diamond mines of South Africa, the uranium mines of the Soviet Union, or the silver mines of Africa.

Though it may surprise you, the richest deposits on our planet lie just a few blocks from your house. They rest in your local cemetery or graveyard. Buried beneath the soil within the walls of those sacred grounds are dreams that never came to pass, songs that were never sung, books that were never written, paintings that never filled a canvas, ideas that were never shared, visions that never became reality, inventions that were never designed, plans that never went beyond the drawing board of the mind, and purposes that were never fulfilled. Our graveyards are filled with potential that remained potential. *What a tragedy!*

There's a wealth of potential in you. You must decide if you are going to rob the world or bless it with the rich, valuable, potent, untapped resources locked away within you.

*Now it is God who has made us for this
very purpose and has given us the Spirit as
a deposit, guaranteeing what is to come*
(2 Corinthians 5:5).

It is a tragedy to know that with over 5 billion people on this planet today, only a minute percentage
will experience a significant fraction of their true
potential. Your potential was not given for you to
deposit in the grave. You must understand the
tremendous potential you possess and commit yourself to maximizing it in your short lifetime. Potential
is not what you have done, but what you are yet able
to do. Potential demands that you never settle for
what you have accomplished.

One of the great enemies of your potential is
success. In order to realize your full potential, you
must never be satisfied with your last accomplishment. It is also important that you never let what you
cannot do interfere with what you *can do*. The greatest tragedy in life is not death, but a life that never
realized its full potential. You must decide today not
to rob the world of the rich, valuable, potent, untapped resources locked away within you.

The field is the world, and the good seed stands for the sons of the kingdom (Matthew 13:38a).

To understand your potential, let us look at one of the most powerful elements in nature...the seed. If I held a seed in my hand and asked you, "What do I have in my hand?" what would you say? Perhaps you would answer what seems to be the obvious...a seed.

However, if you understand the nature of a seed, your answer would be *fact* but not *truth*.

The truth is I hold a forest in my hand. In essence, *what you see is not all there is. That is potential. Not what is, but what could be.*

God created everything with potential, including you. He placed the seed of each thing within itself (see Gen. 1:12), and planted within each person or thing. He created the ability to be much more than it is at any one moment. Thus, everything in life has potential.

He is a God of the potential principle. Everything begins as potential.

God made one person—not a million people. He started with one seed. Then from that one He created another. Then He said, "Bless you (that means, 'You have My permission'). Be fruitful and multiply and replenish the earth."

So we fix our eyes not on what is seen, but on what is unseen. For what is seen is temporary, but what is unseen is eternal (2 Corinthians 4:18).

Potential is always present, waiting to be exposed. It demands that you never settle for what you have accomplished. Don't accept your present state in life as final, because it is just that, a state. Don't be satisfied with your last accomplishment, because there are many accomplishments yet to be perfected. Since you are full of potential, you should not be the same person next year that you are this year.

Never accept success as a lifestyle—it is but a phase. Never accept an accomplishment as the end—it is but a mark in the process. Because you are God's offspring, there are many selves within you that lie dormant, untapped and unused.

Therein lies the tragedy of life. The minute we begin to settle down and be satisfied with what we have, we lose the possibility of revealing what is really inside. Too often we die without exploring our gifts, abilities, and successes. Our thoughts, ideas, and possibilities are not used. We are like batteries in a radio that is never played—our potential is wasted.

*Do not neglect your gift, which was given
you through a prophetic message when the
body of elders laid their hands on you*
(1 Timothy 4:14).

S uppose…

Suppose Shakespeare had died before he wrote
his poems and plays—the potential of *Macbeth*
would have been buried. Suppose Michelangelo had
died before he painted the Sistine Chapel or Da
Vinci the Mona Lisa—the beauty of their paintings
would have been lost. Suppose Mozart had died with
all that music in his bosom.

Suppose Moses had died before he saw the
burning bush…Paul before he met Jesus on the
Damascus Road…Abraham before Isaac was born.
How different the pages of Scripture and history
would be.

Can you imagine how many great works of art,
music, and literature are buried in the graveyard near
your house? Can you imagine how many solutions to
the problems we face today are buried with someone
you knew? People die without getting out their full
potential. They fail to use all that was stored in them
for the benefit of the world.

What would the world have lost if you had not
been born? What will the world lack because you fail
to live out your potential? Will you carry songs, books,
inventions, cures, or discoveries to your grave?

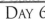

*To know this love that surpasses knowledge—
that you may be filled to the measure of all
the fullness of God* (Ephesians 3:19).

As the time for His crucifixion drew near, Jesus spoke of the potential principle in terms of His life. He compared Himself to a kernel of wheat that falls into the ground and dies (see John 12:23-24). A kernel of wheat, when planted, yields many more kernels. Within Jesus was the potential to bring millions of people to God. That one Seed gave life to many.

There was a time early in his ministry when the apostle Paul said, "I'd like to leave." Though he preferred to die and be with Christ, he knew his purpose in life had not been completely fulfilled. There was yet much fruitful labor for him to do. The benefit of his wisdom would have been lost to the early Church and to us.

Later, near his death, Paul wrote: "Timothy, I've run the race. I've finished the course. I've kept the faith. I've done the work. My award awaits me. I'm ready to die. Keep working after I'm gone" (see 2 Tim. 4:5-7). Everything in life has the potential to fulfill its purpose.

We have different gifts, according to the grace given us (Romans 12:6a).

Perhaps you are wasting your life doing nothing with all you have. God packaged some things in you for the good of the world—use them. We will never know the wealth God planted in you until you bring it up. There's always something in you that we haven't yet seen because that's the way God thinks. Release your ability before you die. Use the power and strength within you for the good of yourself and others. I believe there are books, songs, works of art, businesses, poems, inventions, and investments in you that God intended for His children to enjoy. Don't give up until you have lived out the full extent of your potential, because *you have no right to die with our things*. Don't rob the next generation of the wealth, treasure, and tremendous gifts buried deep within you.

If you want to succeed, strike out on new paths. Don't travel the worn paths of accepted success. No one can climb beyond the limitations of his own belief. Every day sends to the grave obscure men and women whom fear prevented from realizing their true and full potential.

Through Him all things were made; without Him nothing was made that has been made (John 1:3).

Everything in life was created with potential and possesses the potential principle. Creation abounds with potential because the Creator Himself is the potential principle.

When we describe God, we often say He is omnipotent. Omnipotent means that *God is always potent*. Made up of two words: *omni*, meaning "always," and *potent*, meaning "full of power," omnipotent means that God is potentially everything. He has within Him the potential for all that is, was, or ever will be. He is omni-potent or omnipotent.

Everything that was, and everything that is, was in God. That's a very important concept. Everything that was and is, was in God. We have to start with God. Before God made anything, before He created things, there was only God. So before anything was, God is.

God is the root, or source, of all life.

Before anything was, God is.

*In the beginning was the Word, and the
Word was with God, and the Word was God.
He was with God in the beginning. Through
Him all things were made; without Him
nothing was made that has been made. In
Him was life...* (John 1:1-4).

Before there was a beginning, there was God.
Nothing that was created was made without the
Word. In *the Word* was life. *Life* came out of God.
Therefore, before you knew life, life was. Every-
thing you see, hear, smell, taste, and touch was in
God before it came to be. Even what you discern
first existed in God.

Thus if you had talked to God on the highway of
nothingness, you would have been talking to millions
of cows, horses, mountains, trees, limousines, hotels,
and beaches. They all were in God. They were in
Him, but no one saw them. He's always full of the
potential to bring forth what you see. God is pregnant
with the universe. In essence, if you met God on the
highway of nothing, by the corner of nowhere,
before there was anything, and you shook His hand,
you would be shaking hands with *everything*, but
would not know it. You would be with Potential.

By faith we understand that the universe was formed at God's command, so that what is seen was not made out of what was visible (Hebrews 11:3).

God always had everything in Him, but we could not see it. All we now see was once in an invisible state. (Please note that invisible does not mean nonexistent.)

All the buildings we see and the businesses we frequent—people making money and investing money—all that stuff began as ideas. We couldn't see them because they were in somebody's mind. The stores where we shop, everything on the shelves in those stores, began as ideas in someone's mind. They didn't exist before—yet they did.

Although they weren't present in their current form, they existed as lumber and concrete, cotton and wool, steel and motors. Someone had an idea. Through work they put their idea into things that are now visible.

By faith God spat out what was in Him. Whatever you see came from the unseen. Thus, *faith is not the evidence of things that do not exist. It is the evidence of things that are not yet seen.*

Everything we see has always been. It became visible when God spoke it into being. God is the source of life.

My own hand laid the foundations of the earth, and My right hand spread out the heavens; when I summon them, they all stand up together (Isaiah 48:13).

What happened when God spoke at creation? How did He get the invisible to become visible? Let's look at the word spoke.

Spoke was a process. What God spoke into visibility began as an idea in His mind. God first conceived in His mind what He wanted to create. He didn't just say, "I want this." The prophet Isaiah tells us that God created the earth by first planning its foundations (see Isa. 48:13 above). After the plans were in His mind, God spoke them into existence.

God laid the groundwork for the earth and spread out the heavens. He created the sun to shine during the day and the moon and stars at night. He ordered clouds to fill the sky and breezes to blow. He made the waves to roar in the sea. He sent rain to water the earth and grass to cover the hillside. Thunder and lightning were created by His command; hail and sleet were formed by His word. A wool-like blanket of snow He produced for winter; frost and dew He designed.

*By the seventh day God had finished the
work He had been doing; so on the seventh
day He rested from all His work. And God
blessed the seventh day and made it holy,
because on it He rested from all the work of
creating that He had done* (Genesis 2:2-3).

God was full of imagination. He was pregnant
with many thoughts. His thoughts became
ideas, and the ideas became images. Everything that
is came out of God as He *spoke* those images. The
unseen became seen—the invisible became visible.

God didn't create the world by just *thinking* the
whole thing into being. He *worked* it into being.
After creating a plan in His mind, God spoke to
make visible the invisible. (Speaking was one of the
ways He worked.) Through work He created the
world.

For six days God created the heavens and the
earth. On the seventh day He rested.

Spoke must be a fairly serious thing. If God,
who is almighty and all powerful, had to rest after
creation, spoke must have been very hard work.

God was the first One to *sabbat*—He intended
the Sabbath to be a blessing. He knows that life produces work, and work creates the need to rest.

What has been will be again, what has been done will be done again; there is nothing new under the sun (Ecclesiastes 1:9).

The work of God is not complete—He has not delivered all His babies. He will keep on delivering as long as you deliver, because you are the continuation of His deliveries. God can still create. If it doesn't exist in a visible form, God will speak it. He continues to be pregnant with many things.

There's a guy in China right now who is thinking about the idea you thought was yours. Because everything comes out of God, each of you with the same idea all received it from the same Source. Until that idea is transformed by action, God will continue to leak that idea into men and women. Why? Because God is a God of potential. Although *He* is the source of all things, He shares His omnipotent powers with His creation. We, like God, are pregnant with many things. We are full of imagination, having the potential power to be more than we visibly are. There are dreams, visions, plans, and ideas in us that need to be released. God wants us to tap His power and use it, because God made us with potential.

*For this is what the Lord says—He who cre-
ated the heavens, He is God; He who fashioned and made the earth, He founded it;
He did not create it to be empty, but formed
it to be inhabited—He says: "I am the Lord,
and there is no other"* (Isaiah 45:18).

A sculptor works in a very interesting way. I'm an artist of sorts, so I have a bit of an understanding how artists work. One thing I know is that you never argue with an artist during the process. An artist can be very rude if disturbed before the project is completed.

An artist may stop by your house and beg you for a stone you have walked past many times without noticing. Dogs may have been doing stuff on it. But the artist sees something beautiful in that stone beyond what you can imagine.

Months later the artist invites you to his workshop and says, "Do you see that?"

"Do you mean…?"

"Yes. Five hundred dollars, please."

You were sitting on $500. Dogs were doing stuff on $500. You didn't see the potential in the rock.

I praise You because I am fearfully and wonderfully made; Your works are wonderful, I know that full well (Psalm 139:14).

Many people are passed by because others don't see what is in them. But God has shown me what's in me, and I know it is in you too. My job is to say to you: "Can you see what's in you? Do you know your potential? There's a *wealth* of potential in you."

They say Michelangelo used to walk around a block of marble for days—just walking around it, talking to himself. First he would see things in the rock; then he would go and take them out.

Insight like that of a sculptor is seen in the Bible. When the world dumps and rejects you, and you land on the garbage heap of the world, God comes to you. He looks deep within you and sees a person of great worth.

Don't ever let anybody throw you away. You are not junk. God sees things that everybody else ignores. You are worth so much that Jesus went to Calvary to salvage and reclaim you. The Spirit of God connected to your spirit is the only true judge of your worth. Don't accept the opinions of others.

DAY 16

*All the days ordained for me were written
in Your book before one of them came to be*
(Psalm 139:16b).

God looked at Adam and saw a world. He looked
at Abraham and saw nations. In Jacob, a deceiver, He saw a Messiah. In Moses the murderer, God
saw a deliverer.

God saw a king in a shepherd boy. When the
Israelites wanted a king, God sent Samuel to the
home of Jesse. After Jesse had paraded all of his
sons before Samuel, he asked, "Do you have any
other sons?"

Jesse said, "No, well, yes, I do have a boy, just a
little runt who's taking care of the sheep."

"Bring him," Samuel said. Notice that God
chose the son who was working. God chooses busy
people.

Most of us are like Jesse. We look, but we don't
see. Were you the "black sheep" in your family? (You
know God likes sheep.) Has your family told you that
you are a nobody? Have you been told so many times
that you will amount to nothing that you have begun
to believe it? You are the one God is waiting for.

Have you been trying to prove that you are
somebody—and still feel like nobody? Be free from
that today!

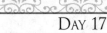

So God created man in His own image, in the image of God He created him; male and female He created them (Genesis 1:27).

When God created the heavens and the earth, He first decided what He wanted to make something out of and then He spoke to that source. When God wanted plants He spoke to the dirt. When God wanted fish He spoke to the waters. When God wanted animals He spoke to the ground. *Whatever God spoke to became the source from which the created thing came.*

All things have the same components and essence as their source. What God created is, in essence, like the substance from which it came. That means plants are 100 percent dirt because they came from dirt. Animals are 100 percent dirt because they came from the ground. If we would take an animal apart, we would come up with genuine dirt. If we would put a plant under a microscope and decipher all the different components, we would find that everything in that plant is in dirt, because the plant is dirt. God called it from the dirt.

Then God said, "Let us make man in Our image, in Our likeness..." (Genesis 1:26a).

————◆————

Not only are all things composed of that from which they came, they must also remain attached to that source in order to live. All things must be maintained and sustained by where they came from. The minute a plant decides it doesn't like the earth anymore, it dies. The minute the fish decide they are tired of water, they die. The minute animals decide, "We don't want to eat any more things made out of dirt," they begin to die.

Thus, whatever God created came from that to which He spoke. All things were created by God's word to a source. The source of the creation also becomes, then, the essence of that creation. All things are composed of whatever they came from and hence contain the potential of that source. That means plants only have the potential of the soil. Animals only have the potential of dirt.

So God created man in His own image, in the image of God He created him; male and female He created them (Genesis 1:27).

God created you by speaking to Himself. You came out of God and thus bear His image and likeness.

For although they knew God, they neither glorified Him as God nor gave thanks to Him, but their thinking became futile and their foolish hearts were darkened (Romans 1:21).

G od has a tremendous problem with idol worship. How can you identify your ability or worth by worshiping a snake, or believing that you will come back as a rat or a roach? You will never know yourself by relating to the creation, only to the Creator. *The key to understanding life is in the* ***Source*** *of life, not in life itself.*

Many of the inventions man has produced would be misunderstood if only the invention were considered and not the intention of the inventor. The man who created the refrigerator had in his mind what it was supposed to be used for. He did not intend it to be a death trap for a curious kid.

The automobile is causing accidental deaths and destruction. But Mr. Ford, who first developed the assembly line to mass produce the automobile, never thought about automobiles that way. He was thinking about transporting people and helping the human race to become a mobile community.

And just as we have borne the likeness of the earthly man, so shall we bear the likeness of the Man from Heaven (1 Corinthians 15:49).

———•———

You will never discover who you were meant to be if you use another person to find yourself. If you want to know who you are, look at God, look at the Creator, not the creation.

Three words describe God. First, God is *omniscient*—He is all knowing. Second, God is *omnipresent*—God is present everywhere. Third, God is *omnipotent*—God is always potent; God is always full of power—He has in Him the potential for everything. From the beginning, God gave that same ability to be potent to all His creation. He planted within each person the ability to be much more than what you are at any one moment. Thus God created you to be omnipotent.

That is not to say we are equal to God. No. But we are always full of potential. Our potential is the dormant ability, reserved power, untapped strength, and unused success God designed into each of us. Your potential is much greater than what you are right now. What we will become is much more than we could ever believe now.

And I tell you that you are Peter, and on this rock I will build My Church, and the gates of Hades will not overcome it (Matthew 16:18).

How you feel or what others say about you is not important. You are who *God* says you are; He sees in you more than you can possibly imagine. Your potential is limited only by God, not others.

God saw in Peter what others failed to see. His given name was *Simon*, which means "meek." (Literally it means "unstable, flaky, leaf.") When Jesus met Simon, he was the flakiest, leafiest man you ever met. He was always going with the wind—changing his mind. But God saw a stone in the leaf. The first time Jesus met Peter, He changed Peter's name from Simon (leaf) to Peter (stone). Although Simon was an unstable guy, Jesus said, "I'm going to change your name. Your name is Peter."

Peter acted like a leaf throughout Jesus' earthly ministry. Still Jesus called him *rock* every morning. Jesus saw in Peter something his mother had not seen. He kept chipping until finally, at Pentecost, Peter's true nature was revealed.

How can you believe if you accept praise from one another, yet make no effort to obtain the praise that comes from the only God? (John 5:44)

God always sees what men and women only *look* at. In a manger, God saw a King…in a servant, a Savior…in a sacrifice, salvation…in a crucifixion, a resurrection. In death, God was working at life; in defeat, He was looking at victory. God looks beyond the surface to the potential deep within. Beyond the immediate troubles God sees success, and He continues to call it forth until what He sees becomes reality.

When we become concerned about our individual lives or the corporate life of our countries, we come up with all kinds of schemes and plans to solve the problem. But the answer is not in a multitude of systems and programs. The answer is right inside of us. It's our attitudes that make the difference. No one can *make you* rowdy or careless or thoughtless. You *are* rowdy and careless and thoughtless because you *choose* to be. Stop being rowdy…stop being careless…stop being thoughtless. Only you can control how you act. You've got the potential to be considerate and sensitive.

"For I know the plans I have for you,"
declares the Lord, "plans to prosper you
and not to harm you, plans to give you hope
and a future" (Jeremiah 29:11).

Too often we believe the lies we are told. We believe that we are worthless. Jesus says, "Not so. I came to show you that you are more than you think you are." You are the image of God.

When we start believing what others say, we are in big trouble. People call us lazy, so we become lazy. People call us careless or stupid, so we become careless or stupid. Watch it! What others look at is not important. Who we are depends on what God sees.

Do you believe that you could meet some of the greatest men and women in the world—in prison? Can you think that way? They made a mistake. But that doesn't invalidate their potential. It doesn't destroy who they can be. When God looks at that person, He doesn't see a murderer; He sees an author or a leader or a great world changer.

Many times God is in disagreement with the people closest to you. Only He knows your true potential. Have you failed? Go to God.

Since you are precious and honored in my sight, and because I love you, I will give men in exchange for you, and people in exchange for your life (Isaiah 43:4).

I have a piece of wooden sculpture in my home that I made many years ago. The sculpture isn't what I first intended it to be because as I was chiseling out the image, part of it was knocked off by too much pressure. Because that part was gone, I could no longer create the image that I had intended. So I looked at the piece of wood and had to rethink how to retain the beauty of the sculpture though I had lost an important part of the wood.

Eventually, I modified my design. The modification is not evident in the finished form. Many people have admired that piece of wood over the years.

That sculpture reminds me of our lives. Parts of our lives have been knocked off by our past, our misjudgments. We've messed up the beauty God intended. But God has taken us—including our marred, chipped, rusted, and knocked off past—and formed us into something beautiful. Allow God to bring beauty out of your mistakes. He can take the thing that seemed impossible to you and form it into something beautiful.

To them God has chosen to make known among the Gentiles the glorious riches of this mystery, which is Christ in you, the hope of glory (Colossians 1:27).

P aul, when writing to the Colossian church, proclaimed that God had chosen to make known a mystery. The mystery is *that Christ is in you*. That is your hope of glory. This suggests, then, that our task is not to get Christ *into* us, but *out* of us. *What God sees when He looks at you is Christ.*

Most of us want to be like Jesus, but God wants us to be like *Christ*. Jesus came to show us what Christ looks like when He takes on human form. God sees Christ in you. That's the hope of glory—*Christ in you*.

The word *image* does not mean "a statue of something." It means "the essence of the being." Christ is the image of God. That means when God created you, He created you in His image, and His image is Christ. That's why the Bible never calls us the Body of Jesus. Jesus was the human manifestation of the heavenly Christ. We humans on earth, with all our fallibilities and weaknesses—God pronounces on us: "You are the Body of Christ."

Until we all reach unity in the faith and in the knowledge of the Son of God and become mature, attaining to the whole measure of the fullness of Christ (Ephesians 4:13).

❝**Y**ou are the Body of Christ." In other words, Christ is in us. God knows He is there. His image is there. So God called us Christ. If we go to God and say, "God, please introduce me to Christ," God will say, "Sure. Here is Christ." But we'll say, "No. I want to meet *Christ*," to which God will reply, "Sure. Here's Christ" as He shows us His Church.

When we want to meet Christ, God will show us the Church. But we can't accept this because we think Christ is in Heaven. No, *Jesus* is in Heaven. *Christ* is sitting in your clothes, living in the body of the believer. Christ is the essence of God—God Himself.

God doesn't need your praise to make Him feel like God. God doesn't need you to tell Him how great He is—He knew it before you ever thought of praising Him. God wants you to know who you are—who you are supposed to look like. He's after the real person buried under the cap of your sin.

But the man who had received the one talent went off, dug a hole in the ground and hid his master's money (Matthew 25:18).

———⬦———

Scientists in the field of human potential have estimated that we use as little as 10 percent of our abilities. Ninety percent of our capabilities lie dormant and wasted.

Consider the life of Abraham Lincoln—the dramatic story of a man struggling to release his potential:

He lost his job in 1832.

He was elected to the legislature in 1834.

He suffered the death of his sweetheart in 1834.

He suffered a nervous breakdown in 1836.

He was defeated for speaker of the state legislature in 1838.

He was defeated for nomination for Congress in 1843.

He was elected to Congress in 1846.

He was defeated for the Senate in 1854.

He was defeated for the nomination for vice president of the United States in 1856.

He again was defeated for the Senate in 1858.

He was elected president of the United States in 1860.

Everything in life was created with potential and possesses the potential principle. The problems of our world go unanswered because potential remains buried.

...The reason the Son of God appeared was to destroy the devil's work (1 John 3:8).

I n the beginning, God created man by speaking to Himself. He took a little bit of Himself and put it into the first man so Adam would be like Him and could share in His life.

But the life God intended for His children was destroyed by their disobedience. Satan's deception and the sin of the man and the woman destroyed the relationship between God and the creatures He had taken out of Himself.

The fellowship of like thoughts and purposes was broken, and our relationship with God became distorted and skewed. Human beings lost their potential to be like the Creator—to know His thoughts and see through His eyes. Through sin, the wealth of God's secret wisdom was buried. The deep things of God became more than we could know or comprehend.

Satan came into our lives to minimize, nullify, and destroy our potential. He has killed, stolen, and destroyed what God planted deep within us. The devil has succeeded in convincing men and women, each with a little part of God, that they are worthless, rotten, incapable people. But Jesus came into the world to reveal who you really are.

Now the serpent was more crafty than any of the wild animals the Lord God had made. He said to the woman, "Did God really say, 'You must not eat from any tree in the garden'?" The woman said to the serpent, "We may eat fruit from the trees in the garden, but God did say, 'You must not eat fruit from the tree that is in the middle of the garden, and you must not touch it, or you will die.'"

"You will not surely die," the serpent said to the woman. "For God knows that when you eat of it your eyes will be opened, and you will be like God, knowing good and evil" (Genesis 3:1-5).

Satan is God's enemy and ours. He is our adversary, out to blind us to the truth of God's love and the wisdom that offers us hope. Whatever steals from you or destroys something that belongs to you is from the enemy. He is a destruction mechanism who comes to destroy, kill, and steal.

What is he destroying? Our potential to be like our Creator. Satan said, "Pick that fruit and be like God." The man and woman were already like God; but by following satan's advice their relationship with God was destroyed.

I know that everything God does will endure forever; nothing can be added to it and nothing taken from it. God does it so that men will revere Him (Ecclesiastes 3:14).

"Father, I want those you have given Me to be with Me where I am, and to see My glory, the glory you have given Me because you loved Me before the creation of the world. Righteous Father, though the world does not know You, I know You, and they know that You have sent Me. I have made You known to them, and will continue to make You known in order that the love You have for Me may be in them and that I myself may be in them" (John 17:24-26).

Satan first deceived Eve by questioning whether God actually said that she could not eat from the forbidden tree. Next, he deceived her by telling her that she could be like God. Satan continued his deception saying, "God is hiding something from you."

He destroyed Adam and Eve's concept of God. God became Someone who was holding something back from them. But Adam and Eve were born related in spirit with God. God *created* them to know Him. Thus, satan stole both man's potential to be like God and his understanding of God.

DAY 31

When he lies, he speaks his native language, for he is a liar and the father of lies (John 8:44b).

———◆———

The deceiver also distorted humankind's self-concept. He said to Adam and Eve: "Look at you. You are naked." So they felt bad about themselves and put on clothes. They covered up their bodies.

Ever since that day, we have become professional "cover-ups." We don't like ourselves. We don't like our physical bodies. I'm too fat, too skinny. My hair is ugly, my eyes are…my lips are…. I don't like my black, brown, red, yellow, white skin. So we try to cover up what we don't like. If our hair is curly, we straighten it. If our skin is too pale, we tan it. Nobody is satisfied with themselves.

This attitude is from the devil. We can't be ourselves because satan has destroyed our appreciation of what God made. Our potential has been distorted. We have accepted satan's ploy to destroy our esteem for the beautiful creation God made us to be.

If you love yourself, you are not going to lower your standards. You will not sell yourself to anybody. You won't allow anybody to buy you—you are too expensive.

Let us discern for ourselves what is right;
let us learn together what is good (Job 34:4).

S atan came to destroy our real intelligence. In the
Garden, a strange word is used in the Hebrew to
talk about knowing. The Bible says Adam and Eve
knew that they were naked (see Gen. 3:7). *Knew*
means they "became physically—or sensually—
aware." Their senses suddenly took on leadership.
Thus the soul became alive without the spirit direct-
ing it. Man began to live from the outside, instead of
the inside. Adam and Eve became aware of their
nakedness. They became aware of the leaves that
could be used to cover themselves. They became
conscious of shame and fear—the things that come
from the outside, from the intellect.

Satan destroyed man's true intelligence, which
is a spiritual relationship with God. When we are
connected with God, our spirits can know anything.
That's why the knowledge God communicates is not
learned. It is discerned. The knowledge of God isn't
found in any book; it's a deeper knowledge. Your real
intelligence is not studied; it is discerned. Wow!

*Commit to the Lord whatever you do, and
your plans will succeed* (Proverbs 16:3).

———❖———

Everything in life was created with potential and
possesses the potential principle. Tragedy
strikes when a tree dies in a seed, a man in a boy, a
woman in a girl, an idea in a mind. For untold millions, visions die unseen, songs die unsung, plans
die unexecuted, and futures die buried in the past.

By destroying our relationship with God, satan
capped off life potential. He continually tries to
destroy any possibility that we might become more
than we already are. He puts teachers in our classrooms to call us stupid. He sends brothers and sisters
to call us dumb and "no good." He gives us parents
who tell us, "You'll never be anything."

Satan sets us up. Satan chops up your self-confidence and slams the door on your potential by
convincing you that you are nothing: "You'll never
rise above your family's status. You'll never go
beyond your neighborhood. You'll never be any
more than your mom and your pa. You don't stand a
chance." The devil has been teaching and preaching
those lies to keep us down. He is very skilled at this
deceptive art.

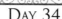

Whoever drinks the water I give him will never thirst. Indeed, the water I give him will become in him a spring of water welling up to eternal life (John 4:14).

Jesus came to destroy satan's lies. He came to free us from those things that retard, distort, and short-circuit everything we are capable of being and doing. He said, *"I am come that they might have life, and that they might have it more abundantly"* (John 10:10 KJV).

OK. That's fine. I have life now.

"But no, that's not enough. I came that you may have an *abundance* of life."

We think life is what we have now. No! In the Greek, the same word is used for *abundance* as is used for *fountain*. Jesus came to take the cap off your well...to unclog the true you...to open up the capacity of who you are and who you can be. We are going to have an oil spill. This thing is going to explode. Jesus didn't come just to take off your well cover. He came to start an explosion of water—a potential welling up and never stopping.

He said, *"Whoever believes in Me, as the Scripture has said, streams of living water will flow from within him"* (John 7:38).

I am come that they might have life, and that they might have it more abundantly (John 10:10 KJV).

Whoever drinks the water I give him will never thirst. Indeed, the water I give him will become in him a spring of water welling up to eternal life (John 4:14).

Jesus came so we can have fountains of life. Man, that's impressive to me!

That means until we get saved, we don't have any life. If you just became born again, you are finally getting back to your real self. All you have done for the last ten years that made you think you were somebody is but a trickle. You haven't changed the world. You haven't changed a person's life for eternity yet. You haven't touched a young child for eternal life yet. You've put clothes on the child's back, but you haven't put anything in his spirit. You haven't done anything yet!

But there is a fountain, an abundance of life, welling up in you so you can do and be something. It begins when you return to your Source through Jesus Christ.

But when He, the Spirit of truth, comes, He will guide you into all truth. He will not speak on His own; He will speak only what He hears, and He will tell you what is yet to come (John 16:13).

Satan is the destroyer who comes to kill and steal and destroy. No one in the world stifles and clogs up and caps your potential like the devil does. He comes with a scheme to make you believe you can be nothing more than you have already been.

Jesus came to destroy this scheme. He came to unclog you and show you your true self. He's the best Destroyer I know. I love this Destroyer.

He who does what is sinful is of the devil, because the devil has been sinning from the beginning. The reason the Son of God appeared was to destroy the devil's work (1 John 3:8).

First John 3:8 says that Jesus came into the world *to destroy* the works of the devil. Jesus came, not to convince God of anything, but to convince us about who we really are. His job is to put us back in touch with what God put within us at birth.

[Christ] *who gave Himself for our sins to rescue us from the present evil age, according to the will of our God and Father* (Galatians 1:4).

———◆———

Most of us have no idea how much talent and potential we possess. The devil delights in capping off our potential. But First John 3:8b says, *The reason the Son of God appeared was to destroy the devil's work.*

What does it mean to destroy the works of the devil? How does Jesus do His job? Jesus reverses what satan has done. For example, when Jesus took sickness from a person's body, He undid the works of the devil. Thus the work of the devil was to put the sickness into that body. When Jesus took away our sins, He destroyed the devil's work of convincing us to sin.

If Jesus feeds hungry people, then it must mean that satan brings poverty and hunger. If Jesus opens the eyes of the blind, then satan must close them. Jesus came to destroy the works of the devil. Whatever He does destroys satan's previous works. Thus when Jesus says, "Everything is possible if you'll just believe" (see Mark 9:23), He is reversing the lies satan has fed us. Jesus came to destroy satan's destruction.

Whoever believes in Me, as the Scripture has said, streams of living water will flow from within him (John 7:38).

Satan tells you that you aren't going to amount to anything. Jesus says, "You can be anything you think." Jesus rips the top right off your capped well. He says, "Go ahead, gush forth."

Thus, a tremendous struggle between two destroyers goes on within us—one destroyer uses a cap, the other a crowbar. Every time the one with the crowbar yanks the top off, the other guy runs around with the cap. The minute we give him a chance, he covers us up again. The struggle is continual. Each day we experience the tension.

Jesus says, "You are saved." Satan says, "You aren't saved." Jesus says, "You are healed." Satan says, "But you still feel the pain." Jesus says, "You are free from drugs." Satan says, "You are hooked for life."

Jesus came to reverse what the devil has done. The devil came to destroy our potential. He distorts, retards, short-circuits, and caps off that which God has placed within us. He uses sin to clog up our potential capacity.

DAY 39

Made us alive with Christ even when we were dead in transgressions—it is by grace you have been saved (Ephesians 2:5).

———————

A re there things in your life that have been hold-ing you back from doing what you should be doing? Are you a potential leader in your community but you're full of alcohol and lying in the gutter? Has cocaine stolen your potential to be the top student in your class? Is your brain all messed up so you can't think clearly any more? Are you in danger of being kicked out of school though you were an A student before you took the stuff? Have you run off with a dumb guy and gotten pregnant? Do you have to drop out of school and give up your visions of becoming a doctor, teacher, scientist, or an agricultural expert? Has sin clogged up your potential?

Did you have a business that was going well, with limitless potential, until somebody said to you, "I want you to sell some drugs for me. You'll make a lot more than you do in this business"? So you became greedy. You went ahead and sold the drugs—only you were caught and now you have a record and your business is destroyed.

Sin clogs our potential. It messes up the plan God has for our lives.

For You know the grace of our Lord Jesus Christ, that though He was rich, yet for your sakes He became poor, so that you through His poverty might become rich (2 Corinthians 8:9).

Sin takes away the "And they lived happily ever after" and replaces it with "And they struggled but didn't make it through the day."

Don't let that be the last chapter in the book God has written on you. God sent Jesus to die for you, not for Himself. Jesus knows *His* potential. He doesn't need to find out what it is. God doesn't have any problem with His potential. He is omnipotent. The problem is that *you* don't know *your* potential. You have been destroyed by the devil, and sin is stunting your growth.

Jesus came, not to die for Himself, but for you, so you could be reconnected with the Source of Life. For this reason Jesus came into the world—to destroy the works of the devil that are holding you down. Jesus came to uncap your well. He gave His life to restore your relationship with God—to give you abundant, flowing, gushing life.

His master replied, "Well done, good and faithful servant! You have been faithful with a few things; I will put you in charge of many things. Come and share your master's happiness!" (Matthew 25:21)

The talents in the Bible story are symbols of the vast store of abilities our Creator has planted within us. The master of the estate entrusts some of his wealth to three of his servants. The first man invests his talent and doubles the wealth. The second servant also doubles what the master had given him. With them the master is very pleased. The master asks the third servant, "What have you done with your talent?"

The servant answered, "I was afraid to misuse the talent, so I carefully hid it. Here it is. I am giving it back to you in the same condition that I received it." In fury the master rebuked his servant, "You wicked and lazy servant. How dare you not use the gifts I gave to you?"

We are responsible for the potential stored within us. Too often our successes prevent us from seeking that which yet lies within us. Success becomes our enemy as we settle for what we have. Refuse to be satisfied with your last accomplishment.

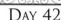
Wisdom is supreme; therefore get wisdom...
(Proverbs 4:7).

Potential is dormant ability. *Dormant* means "that which is, but it is just lying there below its full strength, unused." It is also reserved power, untapped strength, and unused success. Potential is everything that a thing is, that has not yet been seen or manifested. Everything in life begins as potential. All things have the potential to fulfill themselves, because God created everything with potential. There is no fulfillment in life without understanding the reason for being. If we want to know the real potential of something, we first have to know what that thing was created to do.

So if you have a seed in your hand, a kernel of corn, or a pea, you will never get the seed's complete fulfillment until you know that there is a plant inside that seed. It is only as we look beyond the seed to the plant that we understand its true potential.

The same is true of our relationship with God. God created each man with a great wealth of potential. Too often, however, we look only at what we presently have.

Who endowed the heart with wisdom or gave understanding to the mind? (Job 38:36)

———————

The potential of everything is related to its purpose for being. Before we can understand the potential of a thing or person, we first must know the conditions under which it was meant to exist. Thus, the most important thing for you and me is to continually try and find out what our purpose is. Unless we ask ourselves, "What is the purpose for everything in life?" we will die without having experienced or fulfilled our potential. We will miss the wisdom of God in creation.

The apostle Paul describes the wisdom of the world and the wisdom of God:

Where is the wise man? Where is the scholar? Where is the philosopher of this age? Has not God made foolish the wisdom of the world? For since in the wisdom of God the world through its wisdom did not know Him, God was pleased through the foolishness of what was preached to save those who believe. Jews demand miraculous signs and Greeks look for wisdom, but we preach Christ crucified: a stumbling block to Jews and foolishness to Gentiles (1 Corinthians 1:20-23).

Your heart became proud on account of your beauty, and you corrupted your wisdom because of your splendor. So I threw you to the earth; I made a spectacle of you before kings (Ezekiel 28:17).

Before the Fall, lucifer's responsibility in Heaven was to be the music and worship leader. He was designed with the potential not only to lead in music and worship, but also to produce it. Lucifer's body was made with pipes in it so that every time he lifted a wing, a sound came out—music. He never taught an orchestra because the orchestra arrived when he did. As soon as he started fanning his wings, the angels started singing. This guy was a beautiful angel. He had the potential to lead all Heaven into worship and music.

That's why music is such an important part of our world today. Lucifer, the guy running the spirit of the world, is now a cheap musician. The amounts of money the devil uses to support the world's music industry is amazing. Michael Jackson made $220 million in one year. And the Church has difficulty raising even one million.

But God still has the final word. God has put music into the Church and into us. But the reality is, satan's potential is related to his purpose.

Hear this, you foolish and senseless people, who have eyes but do not see, who have ears but do not hear (Jeremiah 5:21).

In First Corinthians, Paul scoffs: "Where are you, those who think you are wise? Is not your wisdom just so much foolishness?" Attacking the supposed wisdom of the world, the apostle declares that it is foolishness. God, in His wisdom, has made the wisdom of the world to be just so much folly (see 1 Corinthians 1:20).

God considers foolishness any wisdom that does not fulfill its original purpose. So if you are wise, but you use your wisdom to steal, God says, "You are foolish." If you are a skillful musician, but you use your talent to create lewdness and sensuality, and to cause people to go into perversion, then God calls that foolishness.

If you know that the power you have to believe was given to you by God, but you prefer to believe there is no God, God calls you a fool. The fool says in his heart, "There is no God." He takes the ability God gave him to believe and uses that power to not believe in God. God says, "That's foolishness!"

For the wisdom of this world is foolishness in God's sight. As it is written: "He catches the wise in their craftiness" (1 Corinthians 3:19).

———◆———

Although God calls the wisdom of the world foolishness (see 1 Corinthians 1:20-23), it is still wisdom. It's a perverted wisdom used by the chief of perverters to blind us to its very foolishness. For who could believe God would use a crucifixion to bring salvation to the world. That is not the way we expect Him to work. We look for miraculous signs and unusual insights to indicate the presence and working of God. What wisdom would choose a poor carpenter to bring the greatest gift the world has ever known? Surely not the wisdom of the world, which looks to the wealthy and the well-educated.

But for those who believe in Jesus Christ, God's apparent foolishness is revealed as true wisdom. The wisest of human thoughts appear puny beside this foolishness of God, and the greatest of man's strengths pales beside Christ's weakness. What is a stumbling block or pure foolishness for those who don't believe in Christ, stands—for the Christian— as a towering source of truth, strength, and hope. *That* is wisdom.

*We do, however, speak a message of wisdom among the mature, but not the wisdom of this age or of the rulers of this age, who are coming to nothing. No, we speak of God's **secret wisdom**, a wisdom that has been hidden and that God destined for our glory before time began* (1 Corinthians 2:6-7, emphasis added).

God has given you a secret wisdom that He placed in you before you were born. He planted within you a potential something—a wisdom to know who you are and what you were created to be and do. That potential something was in God, but He allowed it to leak into you. It's a hidden understanding that follows neither the wisdom of our society nor the insights of our leaders. Unlike the wisdom of the world, which is worthless, God's secret wisdom about you is a priceless jewel.

Many people die without unveiling their wealth of wisdom. They die in total foolishness, without experiencing the life that dwells within. What a pity! They have missed God's secret wisdom. God is not holding back from the world. He is not withholding from us our true potential. We have missed the wisdom God designed before the beginning of time for the honor of others.

"...No eye has seen, no ear has heard, no mind has conceived what God has prepared for those who love Him"—but God has revealed it to us by His Spirit (1 Corinthians 2:9-10a).

You were born with wisdom that literally came out of God.

I know you may find that hard to accept—perhaps you think I am a madman. But the truth is you'll be shocked when you understand who you really are. You have God's secret wisdom, a wisdom that you should be using to discover the earth.

None of the rulers of this world understand it, nor have they ever understood it. Yet, we are constantly dipping into the ways and wisdom of the world to try and solve our present situations. The world does not know the wisdom and potential God has already destined for us.

Your eyes can't see, your ears can't hear, neither can your mind imagine what God intends. It's totally beyond what you can understand without the Spirit revealing it to you. Your eyes and ears and mind cannot help you understand what God prepared for you—lean on the Holy Spirit for revelation.

But God has revealed it to us by His Spirit. *The Spirit searches all things, even the deep things of God* (1 Corinthians 2:10, emphasis added).

*B*ut indicates a change. *But* inserts hope in the midst of hopelessness. Most people do not know what God intends for their lives. They have not seen their secret wisdom, nor have they heard about it. They have never even thought about it because there are certain things we cannot understand unless the Holy Spirit reveals them to us. They are so deep within our potential that we need help to drag them out.

God had those deep things within Him before He made us; He put them into us at birth. But we don't know they exist because sin has blocked the entry way. God struck a well and put wealth in it—a wealth of potential. Wealth is in your bosom. There is wealth in your personality—wealth in your being. But it has been capped off by sin.

Outside God's grace you will never know what is buried beneath. Billions of dollars of wealth are buried within you, but you are not aware of it. You're walking through life, but you don't understand that you are merely the shadow of your potential.

But you will receive power when the Holy Spirit comes on you; and you will be My witnesses in Jerusalem, and in all Judea and Samaria, and to the ends of the earth (Acts 1:8).

When you were born, the cap over your potential was firmly in place. Outside God's grace you will never know what is buried beneath that cap.

We are merely shadows of our potential. In His mercy, God has placed within each of us the answer to this dilemma. After the resurrection of Jesus Christ, God sent the gift of the Holy Spirit. That same Spirit, whom we receive at our new birth, provides the connection between our spirits and God's secret wisdom.

Your capped potential is like a new battery. You came into the world full of the ability to run the whole thing. But you're just sitting there. Your stored power isn't being used. Like a battery that needs acidic water inside it before it can really fulfill its purpose, you need something to unleash the potential locked inside you. The Holy Spirit is the key that allows all the dormant power within you to come to life. Without the filling of the Holy Spirit, you can never function to your fullest potential.

For who among men knows the thoughts of a man except the man's spirit within him? In the same way no one knows the thoughts of God except the Spirit of God (1 Corinthians 2:11).

The Holy Spirit allows all the dormant power within you to come to life.

Have you ever wondered why we have to be born of the Spirit? Why does the Holy Spirit come and connect with our spirits? Think for a moment about your spirit. The deepest knowledge about ourselves comes to us through our spirits—we can't know anything deeper than our spirits reveal. No one knows more about you than you know about yourself; for who can understand a man better than his own spirit (see 1 Cor. 2:11 above)?

If you just got saved, your spirit doesn't know anything about you. Before your new birth in Christ, you were spiritually dead. Before you were saved, your spirit had been paralyzed for 15, 20, or maybe 30 years.

If you are not a Christian, you don't even know who you are, because we are all born spiritually dead. We will never know who we are supposed to be until we accept Jesus as our Savior and receive God's gift of His Spirit.

But, "Let him who boasts boast in the Lord" (2 Corinthians 10:17).

If your spirit doesn't know any more about you than what it has learned since you got saved, look at how little it knows. Do you know where you would be if you had not been saved?

Now don't get me wrong. None of us are perfect yet. We know there is still much that we need to work on—many things that need to be refined. But the more we know about who we are, the more our attitude toward ourselves changes. The minute we realize who we are, we begin to put on kingly clothes. We think, "I'm a child of God now," so we start changing our language. We think, "Wow, I'm a prosperous person," and start expecting things to happen in our lives. As our knowledge about who we are grows, our lives change.

All this is possible because the Holy Spirit pries off the cap on the well of the wealth of our potential. He comes into our lives and goes straight for the things that are clogging us up and dragging us down. Through the power of God, He pulls off that cap and starts to drill.

The words of a man's mouth are deep waters, but the fountain of wisdom is a bubbling brook (Proverbs 18:4).

———————

Some of you have received the revelation of what it cost God to love you. Others of you have not. Some of you are ready to walk into a deeper level of knowledge; others are not.

God beckons you to take another step into a deeper, more relevant knowledge of your potential in Christ—though you may have been saved for years. You need to take this step because you still don't know who you are. Only the Holy Spirit can reveal this truth to you. Your eyes cannot perceive your true potential...your ears cannot hear it... neither can your mind perceive it unless the Holy Spirit gives it to your eyes and your ears and your mind. Until He does, you continue to walk around limiting your potential.

Can we imagine that the source of the deep things of God might be connected to us? Can we go inside God to those things that are deep within Him? Yes, we can! God has given us His Spirit so we can understand all the things He oozed into us.

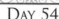
*We have not received the spirit of the world
but the Spirit who is from God, that we may
understand what God has freely given us*
(1 Corinthians 2:12).

It's mind blowing to think that God has given us
His Spirit so we can understand all the things He
oozed into us! There are things about you that you
haven't discovered yet—holy things that only the
Holy Spirit can explain. God reveals His deep things
to you through the Spirit because He knows you
would not believe them if they were simply told to
you through your mind. Your mind cannot possibly
comprehend all that God has prepared for you to be.

That's why God gives you the Holy Spirit. The
Spirit goes deep inside you to capture the wealth of
your potential. He pulls deep from within you the
answers to your spirit's cries, showing you who you
are and why He created you. You will never be fulfilled until you understand why God made you.

Your spirit yearns for the deep things of God
that He has within Him about you. That's why you
have to come to God. You'll never be fulfilled without God, because you are looking for what God has.

Those who live according to the sinful nature have their minds set on what that nature desires; but those who live in accordance with the Spirit have their minds set on what the Spirit desires (Romans 8:5).

Your potential is buried in God. Through the gift of the Holy Spirit, you can reestablish your relationship with God. The Holy Spirit, connected with your spirit, unravels the knots that have bound your thoughts, removes the streaks that have blurred your vision, and clears the debris that has hidden your potential.

Allow God to reveal His secret wisdom concerning you. Conceive with your mind thoughts that never before have occurred to you. Cooperate with the Holy Spirit as He sucks out of God and into you the depths of the riches that God prepared for you. Live the rest of your life building an atmosphere where it is possible for the Holy Spirit to use you as He takes His bucket of hope, dips it deep into the wells of your potential, and pulls it to the top of your senses. Drink deeply, growing in the knowledge of who you really are in God.

*The Lord God formed the man from the dust of the ground and breathed into his nostrils the **breath of life**, and the man became a living being* (Genesis 2:7, emphasis added).

———◆———

Psalm 139 says that God planned each of your days before you were even born. Before you were formed, God knew you. He took great care in creating you. No part of your being was made without God's knowledge and careful concern. God wants each of us. He gives us what no other part of His creation received: His breath of life.

Have you ever felt like you were a mistake? Have your parents told you they wished you had never been born? Are you a child whose parents have told you: "I wish you would have died when you were a baby"?

You may be a bastard, conceived out of wedlock. Being omnipotent, God had the power to prevent your conception. Yet God allowed it because He wanted you to show up. You are here because God wanted you to be born. How you came isn't important. What matters is that you are here. And if you are here, God created you with care (see Ps. 139:13).

My frame was not hidden from You when I was made in the secret place... (Psalm 139:15).

———◆———

King David doesn't describe your mother in Psalm 139—she may have been an alcoholic or a drug addict, a bastard or a prostitute. He is concerned with you. He describes how God knit you together in your mother's womb without describing what that womb was like. The womb in which you were knit together is no longer important. You are important. Your very existence means that God wants you to exist. You are somebody special simply because you were born.

Although some parents feel their baby is a mistake, their thoughts are not true. God planned for all babies to be born. The manner in which the child was conceived may not have been in God's plan, but the child is surely part of God's plan.

Those of you who were brought up in a nice family with a mother and a father who loved you may not understand those who have been put down by their family since birth. It is important for them to know that they are not mistakes. Be patient with them. Help them to see that God designed them long before they were born!

Before a word is on my tongue You know it completely, O Lord (Psalm 139:4).

———•———

God designed you to be somebody. He looked at your unformed body and declared, "This child is good." All His plans for your life were set out long before you took a breath. He wrote out the order of your days before you lived even one day (see Ps. 139:16). There's a book on you. Some chapters God wrote about you haven't even been touched yet.

Some of you are playing around in the index or you have spent years in the table of contents. Perhaps you are 30 years old and you still don't know God's plan for your life. That's playing around on the contents page.

Others jumped ahead of God's plan. Though His design calls for you to be married in chapter 17, you married in chapter 2. You ignored the things God wanted you to learn and experience in chapters 2 through 16 that would prepare you for marriage in chapter 17. Or perhaps you pulled chapter 17 into chapter 2 so that the rest of the book is thrown off.

In order for you to have the opportunity to experience all the chapters God has planned for you, it is important not to veer from God's plan.

You hem me in—behind and before; you have laid your hand upon me (Psalm 139:5).

———◆———

God wants to take you back to the beginning, because His plans far outreach your plans. His design for your life is so great that King David describes it as *vast* (see Ps. 139:17). You are thinking about being a teacher while God wants you to open a school. You have plans to be a clerk while God wants you to own the store. You want to work in a neighboring town while God wants you to go to Africa.

Though you may have messed up God's perfect plan for your life, He graciously offers to write another book for you. It might not be a bestseller in the same way the first book was designed to be, but God gives you the chance to start over. He comes and puts you back in chapter 1 so you can live the many details of His plan. That's what being born again is all about. It's the opportunity to start over— it's finally getting back to the first chapter of God's book on you. God has great plans for you—that's why He gave you life.

Self-acceptance is the key to healthy self-esteem. Accept yourself as God made you. Allow His power to transform your weakness.

The people I formed for myself that they may proclaim my praise (Isaiah 43:21).

Not only did God carefully plan for the details of your life, He also determined how your life would fit into His total plan for humankind. Part of the answer to the why of our birth is revealed in God's desire that we should show forth His glory. The glory of God is the excess of His nature. It's all the potential of our omnipotent God that has not yet been revealed. He's full of so much more than we can think or imagine and He's waiting to use us to realize that potential.

> *Now to Him who is able to do immeasurably more than all we ask or imagine, according to His power that is at work within us, to Him be glory in the church and in Christ Jesus throughout all generations, for ever and ever! Amen* (Ephesians 3:20-21).

God created *you* to bring glory to His name. His predestined plan for *your* life was designed to bring Him glory. Because you share God's omnipotent nature, Jesus said you can do even greater things than He did, if you only believe (see Mark 11:23).

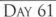
Jesus looked at them and said, "With man this is impossible, but with God all things are possible" (Matthew 19:26).

G od is amazed at our lack of faith in what He has put in us because He knows what we can do. But we don't. And so He says to us: "All things are possible if you'd just believe, dummy." He's always knocking the limits off our lives.

Too often we are not willing to *believe* like God defines believe. God does not say, "Everything is possible if you get the idea." Things don't become reality because we have an idea. We have to believe in the idea. We have to believe we can do it by committing ourselves to it—abandoning ourselves to it—even if it costs us our lives.

God isn't impressed by your dreams alone. Thinking is great. But all things are possible when we believe. Jesus said in Mark chapter 11, *"Whatever you **desire** when you pray, **believe** you'll receive it, and you will have it."*

God's work in creation began with a plan. God conceived in His mind what He wanted before speaking His creations into visible form. By the time God was ready to speak, it was just a matter of taking what was in the plan and putting it on the site.

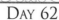
He replied, "...I tell you the truth, if you have faith as small as a mustard seed, you can say to this mountain, 'Move from here to there' and it will move. Nothing will be impossible for you" (Matthew 17:20).

A thought is a silent word, so a word is an exposed thought. Everything in life starts in the thought form—it's a thought first. After it's said, it is no longer a thought. It becomes a word. The next step is an *idea*. An idea is the concept of the thought—it has moved into a reality. Ideas are potentials.

Imagination changes an idea into a plan. If you have an idea it can come and go. You have many ideas in a day—what to cook, what to wear, what to do. Ideas change.

But if an idea develops into an imagination, it means the idea has become a plan. It is still not written or drawn, but it is in your head. Ephesians 3:20 challenges us to believe God is able and willing to do exceeding abundantly, far beyond all we can think or imagine. He dares us to use our imaginations.

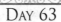
For nothing is impossible with God (Luke 1:37).

My son and I were out in the yard playing bat and ball. I was throwing the ball to him and he was swinging the bat, but kept missing the ball. Finally he became really upset and said, "I can't do that," to which I replied, "There's nothing named 'can't.'" Slowly he repeated after me, "There's nothing named 'can't.'" Then I said, "Hold the bat," and I threw the ball. He hit the ball and then said, "There's nothing named 'can't'!"

Several days later when I stopped by home to drop off my daughter, my son came running and wanted to play basketball. When I said that I had to go to the office, he said, "There's nothing named 'can't.'"

Do you see the point? If he begins to think that way at four years of age, this world is in for a winner. Too often we fail because we think there are things we cannot do. The people who change the world are people who have taken *impossible* out of their vocabularies.

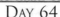

I can do everything through Him who gives me strength (Philippians 4:13).

The apostle Paul, when looking back over his years in the Lord's service, stated that he could do all things through Christ who strengthens him. The Greek terminology for *strengthen* does not mean we are weak and God comes and props us up. Paul's words literally mean: "Christ who continues to infuse me with ability."

Thus Paul is saying: "I can do all things through the potential of Christ who infuses me with the ability to do all things." This strength is not a strength that comes once in a while, but it is a continual ability that is infused into us because we are connected to Christ. Our potential is not limited to doing *some* of the things God asks us to do. We can do *all things*—whatever we believe and desire to do for God. We can do this because the ability to do so is already deposited in us. The basis for this deposit of Christ's ability goes back to God's work in creation.

God is the source of all potential; so your potential is as great as God's potential. The limit of your potential is God.

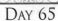
As you do not know the path of the wind, or how the body is formed in a mother's womb, so you cannot understand the work of God, the Maker of all things (Ecclesiastes 11:5).

A creator will not call forth from his creation something he did not put into it. If, for example, the Ford Motor Company wanted to build a car with an engine that was supposed to have a certain degree of horsepower to get up to 200 miles per hour, they would create a car with enough spark plugs and pistons and other things to run at that speed. They build into the car the ability to produce 200 miles per hour. They are calling forth from the car, or demanding of it, what they created it to produce.

If you want to fly from Nassau to Chicago, you depend upon the expertise and knowledge of others to assure you that you will get there. You may look at the airplane and say, "This thing will never get me to Chicago," but what you believe doesn't really matter because you are not the creator of either the airplane or the flight route. The potential of a thing is determined by the demands placed upon it by the creator.

But the Scripture declares that the whole world is a prisoner of sin, so that what was promised, being given through faith in Jesus Christ, might be given to those who believe (Galatians 3:22).

The potential of a thing is determined by the demands placed upon it by the creator. This is the most amazing thing I have ever discovered about potential. A creator will not call forth from his creation something he did not put into it.

Whenever God demands something of you, don't ask whether you can do it. When you pick up the Bible and read that you can do anything if you believe, don't argue that you can't. God believes (in fact He knows) that whatever you believe hard enough, strong enough, and commit to enough can come out of you because He put it in you. Your potential, like that of any other creation, is determined by the demands of your Creator.

God mercifully says to you, "If there are any defects, return to the Manufacturer." Isn't that a blessing? If you aren't working out, take your stuff back to the Chief. The Chief will work it out. "Come unto Me," God says. "I'm the only One who can fix you." God already has guaranteed what you can do.

*And His incomparably great power for us
who believe. That power is like the working
of His mighty strength* (Ephesians 1:19).

When God says, "Love your enemies," don't
start listing reasons why you can't. The ability to love is built in…it's there…no excuses. God
wouldn't ask for it if it wasn't available. He wired
you to produce everything He demands.

Whenever God gives you a responsibility, He
also gives you the ability to meet that responsibility.
In other words, *whatever God calls for, He provides
for.* If God tells you to do something, He knows you
can do it. So don't you dare tell God that you can't.
Just because He told you to assume that responsibility means He knows you can do it. The problem isn't
that you *can't*, it's that you *won't*.

Whether you use the ability God has deposited
within you is totally up to you. How well you assume
the responsibilities God gives you is not so much a
question of how much you do, but rather how much
of the available power you use. What you are doing
is not near what your ability is. What you have
accomplished is a joke when compared with what
you can accomplish as you work with the power of
God (emphasis on *work*).

There is surely a future hope for you, and your hope will not be cut off (Proverbs 23:18).

The Bible tells us: If you can conceive it, you can do it. Obviously God is trying to communicate that you *can* do anything you can *think*. If God has given you a dream or vision that you can conceive, the fact that you can conceive it means you can do it. It doesn't matter if it's never been done—if you think it, you can do it. Likewise, if you never think it, you can't do it. When a thought comes from God, He allows you to think only what you can do. If He doesn't allow you to think it, He knows you can't do it.

Think about the things you've been thinking recently. The fact that you thought them means you can do them. Now don't get me wrong. Thinking doesn't get it done. Thinking implies you can do it. See yourself doing the thing in your thoughts. Make your thought into an idea, and your idea into an imagination. Take that imagination and document it into a plan. Then go to it (of course with the proper rest periods). Put your plan into action. If you thought it, you can do it.

But the fruit of the Spirit is love, joy, peace, patience, kindness, goodness, faithfulness, gentleness and self-control... (Galatians 5:22-23).

Each of the fruit of the Spirit is an attribute of God. God unconditionally says, "They are you." God knows you have love. He knows you have joy—it doesn't matter what you are going through. God knows you have joy down there inside you, because Christ is joy.

Peace. How do you explain that? I used to think it meant the Prince of Peace. "Hello, Prince." I always thought: "Others have the peace. Give me some, Jesus." But that's not what the Bible teaches. The Bible says you have *peace*. When you are unhappy and everything is going wrong, God says, "Have peace." Peace is not a gift; it's a fruit. Joy is not a gift; it's a fruit. If God has it, you have it.

As Romans 5:5 puts it: *"...God has poured out His love into our hearts by the Holy Spirit...."* After you return to God, the Holy Spirit brings love back to your heart. He ignites the stuff that has been in your heart all along. It's not that you can't love; you just don't want to love. Love isn't a something you obtain, because you already have it. That's why you can love your enemies.

Then God said, "Let Us make man in Our image, in Our likeness, and let them rule over the fish of the sea and the birds of the air, over the livestock, over all the earth, and over all the creatures that move along the ground" (Genesis 1:26).

Your purpose for being is to dominate the earth.

God says, "Dominate the earth."

And you quickly reply, "But, but, but…"

Still God says, "Dominate the earth. I have created you to dominate the earth. I demand that you control, rule, govern, dominate, subdue, and subject this planet."

God wouldn't have made that demand if you couldn't do it. He wired you to dominate the planet. You have the potential to dominate Earth because God placed within every human being the ability. That is a very serious domination. You dare not complain when you are dominated by the earth (instead of the earth being dominated by you) because God has placed within you the capacity to do whatever He asks. Don't you dare tell God that you cannot do it. He did not give you the responsibility without also giving you the ability. He created you with the ability to dominate the earth.

For everyone born of God overcomes the world. This is the victory that has overcome the world, even our faith (1 John 5:4).

One morning I said to my little boy as he ran into the room and jumped on me, "You know, I'm holding in my hands all you haven't been yet." Although he didn't understand much of what I was saying, I was thinking about the vast amount of potential that lay within him just waiting to be used. Potential is like that. It's all you can be and become that you haven't yet experienced. Think about it. Potential is all you are capable of being or doing or reaching. You haven't done it yet, but you can do it.

When God tells you to dominate everything, He is pointing to a potential that lies deep within you. You can overcome every habit, because God has clearly stated that you can. Some of you have resolved that you are hooked for life. That's a lie. The problem isn't that you *can't* control your habit; the problem is that you *won't*.

I have news for you—good news. You have what God demands. God will never demand anything He's not already provided for. God commanded you to dominate the earth, and the truth is you *can*.

God blessed them and said to them, "Be fruitful and increase in number; fill the earth and subdue it. Rule over the fish of the sea and the birds of the air and over every living creature that moves on the ground" (Genesis 1:28).

No one needs to be ruled by cocaine or marijuana. Nobody needs to be the victim of alcohol or money. They are all but leaves from the trees that we are supposed to be dominating. The only way to escape these and other dominating habits is to understand your purpose for being. God did not create you to be dominated by sex or chemicals. He did not create you to be *controlled* by anything. He created you so *you could control* the earth.

God looks under all the junk and says what He sees: "You are pure. You are the righteousness of God in Christ Jesus." He's trying to expose the real you He already sees.

When you wake up tomorrow morning, stretch, look in the mirror, and say: "You successful thing you." That's who God sees. Go ahead. Stretch. Enjoy the success that is waiting for you.

Do not conform any longer to the pattern of this world, but be transformed by the renewing of your mind. Then you will be able to test and approve what God's will is—His good, pleasing and perfect will (Romans 12:2).

When God told His people: *"For My thoughts are not your thoughts, neither are your ways My ways"* (Isa. 55:8), He was not saying He doesn't want our ways and thoughts to be like His. God was telling us: "Your thoughts and ways are not like Mine, but I'm trying to get them like Mine." God wants us to have a mind like His. He told us through the apostle Paul to be transformed by the renewing of our minds. He wants you to know and obey His will—doing what is pleasing and acceptable in His sight (see Rom. 12:2 above).

Too often we wake up and say: "Oh, God. It's Monday." God says: "You're not thinking like Me. This is a day I made just for you. Come on, let's go out there and give 'em Heaven." Give 'em Heaven? Yeah, that's right. There's a world out there that is hurting. Let's go give them Heaven.

Believe His assessment of your potential.

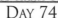
What is man that You are mindful of him,
the son of man that You care for him?
(Psalm 8:4)

W e have allowed the world around us to determine our potential. Teachers say to students:
"You are a C student." The student then goes around
believing that, and he becomes an average student
for the rest of his life—an average person even. He
becomes an average husband. She becomes an average wife. We become average parents and average
children with average IQs. When we turn out to be
average, our parents say: "Well, honey, you have my
genes." No. We received your attitude transmitted to
you from that teacher.

Shake off what people call IQ. *IQ* means "Intelligence Quotient" and is based on tests taken as a
youngster—sometimes labeling children as "D students" or "C people."

Unfortunately, people believe what they are told
based on those tests. Fortunately, there are thousands
of examples in history of people who shed their
labels and turned out to be some of the world's greatest leaders. Your potential has nothing to do with
those tests. Only God determines your potential.

After that, we who are still alive and are left will be caught up together with them in the clouds to meet the Lord in the air. And so we will be with the Lord forever (1 Thessalonians 4:17).

———————

One day as I was talking with the Holy Spirit, He said to me, "Myles, what are you?"

I said, "Spirit."

He said, "Yea! You got that down! Do you know that spirits cannot die?"

I said, "This is true."

Then He said, "Why do humans think in terms of time only? I came back to earth to introduce humans to eternity."

I said, "Whoa!"

Then the Holy Spirit showed me how God had designed us to live forever. He said, "If you have to live forever, which you will, what are you going to do? God intended you to live forever because spirits never die. And you have to live forever being fulfilled. God never makes anything without a purpose. So you are designed to live forever and you've got to be fulfilling your purpose in life. God had to make sure He stored enough in you to last forever so you will never get bored." That blew my mind.

We are going to live forever.

Lord, You have been our dwelling place throughout all generations (Psalm 90:1).

There is no retirement in the Bible. Why? Because God knows you have eternity to go just like He does. God wants you to assist Him in creating and developing and dominating and ruling forever and ever and ever. That's a long time. The wealth of your potential is so rich it requires an eternal life to bring it out.

We are not going to be in Heaven for a million years bowing down around a throne. God doesn't have an ego problem. He doesn't need us to tell Him how nice He is. In fact, He was nice without us. We are the only ones made in His image, and look what we did. God was better off without us. He doesn't need our praises.

God has placed enough potential in you to last forever. Try to do as much now as you can. Pack as much as you can into the 70 to 100 years you have here. Go for it. Go for a hunk of gold. Go for the mountain that has the gold in it. Go for the whole thing. Because if you can think it, you can do it. God is the limit of your ability.

Therefore I tell you, whatever you ask for in prayer, believe that you have received it, and it will be yours (Mark 11:24).

The people who are blessings to humanity are people who believe there is an ability inside them to accomplish something. Though they may not know *exactly* what they can do, they *try* because they believe they can accomplish something.

One day as a youth, I was in my neighbor's yard and her vicious dog suddenly appeared. I had just touched down after climbing the fruit tree, and as I considered the distance between the fence, the dog, and myself, I knew I had to make a run for it. I ran toward the fence with the dog close behind me. As the fence came closer, all I could think was "jump." When I landed, I was safely on the other side of the fence.

I thank God for that dog. He was a blessing in my life. I discovered that day there is a lot more potential in me than I realized!

The same is true for you. You aren't doing more because no one has challenged you. You will accomplish it if you set out to do it.

...If anyone serves, he should do it with the strength God provides, so that in all things God may be praised through Jesus Christ. To Him be the glory and the power for ever and ever. Amen (1 Peter 4:11).

I am reminded of a young fisherman who decided, "I'm going to take a chance and try to walk on water." One night as the disciples were crossing Lake Galilee it was hard rowing. As they struggled, a man came walking toward them on the water. In fear they cried out, "It's a ghost." When He spoke to them, the disciples recognized Jesus. Peter said, *"Lord, if it's you...tell me to come to you on the water"* (Matt. 14:28). When Jesus said "Come!" Peter had the guts to respond.

I believe every one of those disciples could have walked on water. The potential was in them even as it was in Peter. But only Peter succeeded, because only Peter had the guts to say, "If you challenge me, I'll take your challenge." Although we may laugh or criticize Peter for sinking, none of us has ever walked on water. He's the only guy who can say in Heaven when we get there, "I walked on water. What did you do?"

And God is able to make all grace abound to you, so that in all things at all times, having all that you need, you will abound in every good work (2 Corinthians 9:8).

God has promised that He can do far more than you can think or imagine. His power is available to you. Is that power working in you? Are you saying to God: "I've got some power, now work it for me. Give me something to do"?

God has given you a skill or ability the world needs. He has been waiting for your birth. Perhaps He planted within you a unique ability to work for life. Imagine a dead baby turning purple in your hand. Others are thinking "undertaker," but you know that God has given you a potential to restore life. You believe God and pray, by the power of His Spirit, "God, this dear baby must live." Even though someone might overhear you, and that makes your prayer all the more difficult, you tap into the potential God planted deep within you and believe for the baby's life.

God has given you a skill or ability the world needs. Don't waste that gift. Give your potential some responsibility.

I have told you these things, so that in Me you may have peace. In this world you will have trouble. But take heart! I have overcome the world (John 16:33).

People who have made changes in history are those who have told the odds it is impossible to stop them. Don't throw yourself away—don't let anyone else throw you away because you are up against some odds.

I think about President Roosevelt in a wheelchair. Did you ever think an invalid could be the president of one of the greatest nations on earth? Suppose you end up in a wheelchair next year with all the brains you have right now. Will you quit? Is your dream related to your body? Some would get depressed and say, "Oh, life didn't work out for me," allowing their dreams to die in the chair.

Don't give up because you are physically handicapped. Don't give up if you are facing great odds. Your potential is not determined by whether you can see the fine print of a book, walk across the street, or lift heavy objects with both hands. Your potential is not destroyed because your mother is an alcoholic, your father is a junkie, or you have no parents at all. Don't give up. Beat the odds.

And observe what the Lord your God requires: Walk in His ways, and keep His decrees and commands, His laws and requirements, as written in the Law of Moses, so that you may prosper in all you do and wherever you go (1 Kings 2:3).

Ben Johnson is an athlete from Canada who set many world records, including the 1987 world record in the 100-yard dash at 9.83 seconds. In 1988 he broke his own record, winning the race in 9.79. But that year he used steroids. We will never know his potential. There was no reason for his shortcut. He had a world record.

I picked up a magazine and noticed an advertisement: "doctorate degree? Call us." People who responded to an ad like that didn't allow themselves the chance to see what they could really do. They may have the degree, but they didn't fulfill the requirements.

There are no shortcuts to developing your potential. You will never know what you might have achieved if you use a crutch to get there. You'll never know what you may have learned if you get a degree without fulfilling the requirements. Shortcuts negate potential. They destroy the possibilities God planted within you.

With this in mind, we constantly pray for you, that our God may count you worthy of His calling, and that by His power He may fulfill every good purpose of yours and every act prompted by your faith (2 Thessalonians 1:11).

After God created Adam, He gave him a job. God knew Adam's potential to name all the animals would never be released unless it was challenged. Potential must be exercised to be fulfilled. Demands must be made on potential if it is to be released and fulfilled. God has given you potential. Unless you make demands on it, you will die with it. Unless you venture to try things you've never done before, you'll never experience the wealth that lives within you.

The greatest works in the world will be done by people who don't care who gets the credit. Success requires striking out on new paths. Genius is 1 percent inspiration and 99 percent perspiration. There are four steps to the accomplishment of your dream: Prepare prayerfully. Plan purposefully. Proceed positively. Pursue persistently. Failure is the path of least persistence.

If the Lord delights in a man's way, He makes his steps firm; though he stumble, he will not fall, for the Lord upholds him with His hand (Psalm 37:23-24).

No one can climb beyond the limitations he has placed on himself. It is courage that counts—courage and the willingness to move on. A great deal of talent is lost to the world for want of a little courage. Every day sends obscure people to the grave, whom fear and timidity have prevented from making their first attempt to do something. Never tell a person that something can't be done, because God may have been waiting for centuries for someone ignorant enough to believe that the impossible could be possible.

Success is never final—failure is never fatal.

One good thing about failure is that it is proof that you tried. The greatest mistake you can make is to be afraid of making one. Challenge your potential. Demand things of yourself that are beyond what you have already done. Expect more from yourself than the accomplishments that are easily within your reach. The limit of your potential is God. It is better to attempt a thing and fail, than to never try and not know you could succeed.

For He knows how we are formed, He remembers that we are dust (Psalm 103:14).

A grapevine is an interesting plant. The vine, which is the thick wooden part running from the ground up the pole, is the only part of the plant that contains life ability. None of the life is in the branches; all of it is in the vine. There is no life in the little green things you see on the side with the grapes hanging on them. They are getting their life from the vine. They have no root in themselves.

If you were to break one of those green branches off and plant it in the ground, it would never grow because it has no life ability in it. Each small branch has to depend on the life flowing up and down the great branch, the vine, to give it life. Thus the branches cannot live without the vine. The relationship of the vine and its branches is reflected throughout God's creation.

Life is not possible when a thing is separated from its source.

For in Him you have been enriched in every way—in all your speaking and in all your knowledge (1 Corinthians 1:5).

Everything God creates has the same components as its source.

When a plant dies, it goes back to where it came from—it quickly decays and you can't find it. When an animal dies, it goes back to where it came from—you can't find it. When a person dies, the person goes back to the spirit realm.

Wherever something comes from, it has to remain attached to that source in order to fulfill itself. All created things must be maintained by their source. The potential of everything is related to source; everything must be attached to its source if it is going to fulfill its potential.

Our life depends upon our Source. We came out of God and contain a measure of His ability. But our only hope of fulfilling that ability lies in God. We must be hooked up with God if we are going to tap any of our true potential. Jesus came to bring us back to God so God's original intention when He took man out of Himself could be fulfilled. Thus the key to your full potential is staying related to God.

*I am the **true vine**, and my Father is the gardener* (John 15:1, emphasis added).

As a plant cannot fulfill its potential without being in relationship with the soil, so you cannot fulfill your true potential without being related to God. Jesus calls Himself the *true vine* because there are a lot of other vines around to get hooked into: education, philosophy, science, even religion.

To reach their potential, the branches and the vine need the attention of the gardener. The gardener brings as much life as possible out of the vine. Often he prunes the vine because he knows there is more life down in the roots. Cutting off the old leaves that stop the vine from producing its full potential, the gardener starts to clean up the vine.

Are there some old leaves in your life that have been hanging around for 5, 10, or 15 years? Do you need to quit a habit or two so your life more truly reflects the potential of the One who made you? Prune your life through discipline and obedience to God, who desires your potential to be maximized. Remember, all God's commands and laws are given to maximize your performance and free your potential.

And this is love: that we walk in obedience to His commands. As you have heard from the beginning, His command is that you walk in love (2 John 1:6).

When God placed Adam and Eve in the Garden of Eden, He said, *"You are free to eat from any tree in the garden; but you must not eat from the tree of the knowledge of good and evil, for when you eat of it you will surely die"* (Gen. 2:16-17). God gives you freedom, but He also puts some limitations on you. Whenever you violate your limitations, you are in rebellion against God. The only limitations of your potential are violations of God's Word. That's a tremendous freedom. You are free to do anything within the context of God's Word.

God comes into your life with pruning shears to free you from your disobedience and rebellion. He comes to take out those things that are stopping you from developing and growing and obeying. He wants you to enjoy the freedom of obedience and life within His limitations. God trims the useless and dead wood from your life so you can draw from Him the fresh fullness of your potential.

Remain in Me, and I will remain in you. No branch can bear fruit by itself; it must remain in the vine. Neither can you bear fruit unless you remain in Me (John 15:4).

———•◆•———

Jesus is the true vine. You are a branch. If you remain in Christ and Christ in you, you will bear abundant fruit. If you do not remain in Christ, you are like a branch that withers and is thrown away. No branch can bear fruit if it is not attached. It starts going in the opposite direction. No matter how talented or gifted you are, you will never be truly fulfilled and successful apart from a personal relationship with your Creator-Source.

The secret to a happy, productive life is remaining attached to your Divine Source. If you abide in Christ, His Word will abide in you. You can ask whatever you wish and it will be given to you. God will provide from the depths of His grace…freely, abundantly, victoriously. God is always waiting to help you live a full, fruitful, complete life. From His storehouse of riches, God will supply all you can imagine and more because *He wants you to fulfill your potential.*

*If you remain in Me and My words remain
in you, ask whatever you wish, and it will
be given you* (John 15:7).

Jesus' words are almost frightening—*whatever
you wish*. God will give you whatever you ask for
so long as you remain in Him. What a promise!
When you open your life completely to God, the
Holy Spirit's crowbar firmly resists satan's attempt
to recap your well. The wealth of your potential
becomes limitless and free. Whatever you imagine
will be done, because God won't allow you to think
it unless you can do it.

What kind of life are you living? Are you in
tune with Christ or are you off doing your own
thing? Is there sin clogging up your pipes, prevent-
ing you from accomplishing and achieving your
maximum ability? Are you constantly hustling,
struggling to make your way in the world? If you
are, you probably have not become a disciple of the
Risen Christ. You see, being a Christian is not
enough to fulfill your potential. The word *Christian*
was given to us by pagans. Jesus never called us
"Christians." This term was given to the disciples in
the early Church by the pagans in Antioch.

Then a teacher of the law came to Him and said, "Teacher, I will follow you wherever you go" (Matthew 8:19).

Only a disciple experiences full potential. Because his greatest desire is to know and resemble the Master, he spends hours listening to His words. He seeks new visions, revelations, and understandings concerning the Master's life and who He calls His disciples to be.

I do not consider myself to be great or superior to anyone else, but I decided at the age of 14 that I wanted to understand everything that God has prepared for me. I invested hours in the Word of God—large chunks of time…sometimes half a day. After 15 years, God said to me, "That's still not enough. Follow Me."

Don't fall for the limitations of the world—the lies and deceptions of the lower nature. Find your Source and get connected. Then stay connected. God has chosen you to go and bear fruit—fruit that will last. Abide in Christ, and the Father will give you whatever you wish. Refuse to live below your privileged potential. Drink deep from the Vine and let your life feed others.

In a desert land He found him, in a barren and howling waste. He shielded him and cared for him; He guarded him as the apple of His eye (Deuteronomy 32:10).

In discussing the awesome task of tapping our true and full potential, it is essential that we come to appreciate how important each one of us is and how special we are to God. If you were aware of how much power and worth you have, the first thing that would be affected would be your attitude toward yourself.

Many of us have a difficult time projecting a good attitude toward others because we feel bad about ourselves. Great positive thinkers and personal motivators, along with psychologists, all agree that if you feel good about yourself, then your attitude toward others will be influenced by that attitude.

On the contrary, what we are discussing here is something different. We are talking here about a fact grounded in truth and reality, and established by the One who created you. Your worth, value, and potential have all been given by God, and there is no formula, test, or scheme to measure the full extent of these qualities and abilities.

And I heard, as it were, the voice of a great multitude, as the sound of many waters and as the sound of mighty thunderings, saying, "Alleluia! For the Lord God Omnipotent reigns!" (Revelation 19:6 NKJV)

*E*verything that is was in God. In essence, everything that exists came out of God or proceeded out of His creative Spirit. He is the Source of everything. The first verse of the Book of Genesis introduces God as the Creator of all things, *"In the beginning God created the heavens and the earth"* (Gen. 1:1).

God began the beginning. He did not start when start got started—He started start. There was no beginning without God. He is the Source, Creator, and Sustainer of everything. Nothing exists that He did not create. If it does not exist, it is because He has not yet created it. He is the ultimate Source of everything. Anything and everything that comes after the beginning has to come out of God.

Before anything existed, God had it in Him. That is the reason we ascribe to God alone the term *omnipotent*. God does not only *have* potential; He is potential—and the Source of all potential. The source of all potential is in the Omnipotent One.

DAY 93

Far above all rule and authority, power and dominion, and every title that can be given, not only in the present age but also in the one to come (Ephesians 1:21).

Principle: the potential of a thing is related to its source.

This principle is evidenced by all manufacturers who enclose a *manual* with their product detailing the expected performance and potential of their product. The manufacturer wants you to read the manual before using the product so it can tell you what demands to make on the product.

Your true ability and potential should not be measured by the limitations of an academic test or an Intelligence Quotient score. Nor should it be determined by the social, cultural, economic, and educational "norms" of your society. Society did not create you. You are not a product of your culture. You are not the offspring of your economy. You were not created by the Department of Education. Therefore, none of these has the right to determine how much potential you really possess. If you want to know how much potential you have, first discover who created or manufactured you. Then check the demands He is making upon your life. Whatever He is demanding of you, *you can do*.

Do you not know that your body is a temple of the Holy Spirit, who is in you, whom you have received from God? You are not your own (1 Corinthians 6:19).

Principle: the potential of a thing is determined by the demands made on it by the one who made it.

People who change the world and significantly impact humanity are those who have discovered the limitless nature of their potential. If you are going to realize and maximize your full potential, you will have to understand the true nature of your potential. But to do this, you must first understand the process of your creation and the Source from which you came.

If you examine the Scriptures from Genesis chapter 1, you will discover that whenever God wanted something He spoke to the material substance from which He wanted it made. He wanted plants to be made out of soil or dirt, so He spoke them out of the earth. That is why, when a plant dies, it decomposes back to the soil. He spoke the stars from the gasses in space; therefore stars are 100 percent high density nuclear gas explosions. When a star "dies," it dissipates into gasses and returns to its original state.

This is how you can recognize the Spirit of God: Every spirit that acknowledges that Jesus Christ has come in the flesh is from God (1 John 4:2).

Man does not have a spirit, he is spirit—because of the Source from which he came. The process-principle of creation introduces us to principles that we must understand if we are to fully appreciate the nature of our potential. These principles are evidenced in nature and are scientifically sound. They are as follows:

1. When God wants something He speaks to what He wants it made out of.
2. Each thing that exists is composed of the same material substance as where it came from. It is a composite of its source.
3. Each thing that exists has to be sustained and maintained by where it came from.
4. The potential of a thing cannot be fulfilled without being related to its source.

These principles are clearly demonstrated by God's system of creation in nature. This holds true for humans also: Man (spirit) came out of God (source) and must remain related (attached) to God (his source) in order to live.

Jesus answered, "I am the way and the truth and the life. No one comes to the Father except through Me" (John 14:6).

As the plants need dirt and the fish need water, so humankind needs God. If we are to realize and maximize our true potential, a relationship with God is not an option. It is a necessity. If we are to become all we are purposed to be, God is not an alternative but a requirement.

This point is crucial because it helps us understand the ultimatums of Jesus and the emphatic demands of God the Father. The call of the Kingdom is not that we *should* be born of the *spirit*, but that we *must* be born of the *spirit*. Jesus didn't say, "I am *a way*," but *"I am the way"* (John 14:6). It was also He who said, *"I am the vine; you are the branches. ...apart from Me you can do nothing"* (see John 15:2-8).

This principle is also communicated in God's command to Adam in Genesis. Sin, therefore, can be understood as man's declaration of independence from his Source. This is evidence that no matter how far man progresses or how much he accomplishes, he can never experience his full potential without a personal relationship with God, his Source.

May God Himself, the God of peace, sanctify you through and through. May your whole spirit, soul and body be kept blameless at the coming of our Lord Jesus Christ (1 Thessalonians 5:23).

Man is a triune being created after the image and likeness of his Creator-Source. He consists of three distinct yet intricately related dimensions. Each dimension is designed to fulfill a specific purpose in God's plan for His creation. But the potential of each dimension cannot be understood apart from its Source. Let us now take a closer look at each part of man and explore the untapped potential that lies buried there.

In man's pursuit of knowledge about his world and environment (through the disciplines of science), he reaches the general conclusion that the magnificent mystery of the human body still stands at the apex of all natural forms of creation. Specialists continually study the physiological potential of the human body—to adjust itself to varying environmental changes; to defend itself against disease, danger, or threat; to maintain its stamina under physical exertion.

The human body has been described as 80 percent water (fluid), with a degree of calcium, fiber, and tissue. But to fully appreciate the true potential of the human body, we must understand the *purpose* for its creation.

Therefore do not let sin reign in your mortal body so that you obey its evil desires (Romans 6:12).

————◆————

To understand the purpose of the body, we must understand the purpose for humankind. When God created man, He created him a *spirit* being with a *physical* house (body). Then God placed him on the physical earth. God purposed and intended to rule and dominate the physical realm from the invisible realm through the agency of humankind. In essence, God desired to control the *seen* from the *unseen* through the *unseen* living in the *seen* on the *seen*. Therefore, the triune nature of man is designed for the following purposes:

1. Man's spirit: To relate to God (the spirit world).
2. Man's soul: To relate to the mental realm (intelligence).
3. Man's body: To relate to the physical environment (the earth).

The human body was specifically designed to relate to and pick up the earth or physical realm. For this reason, our five senses are specifically designed to "pick up" our natural environment. Our powers of sight, touch, hearing, smell, and taste are all related to the natural, physical world. However, God never intended man to be controlled or limited by his physical body.

Since we live by the Spirit, let us keep in step with the Spirit (Galatians 5:25).

———————

Man's original state in the Garden of Eden, before the Fall, was one of perfect union and fellowship with God. God designed man to be *led* by his spirit, not *driven* by his environment. Man was intended to live through spiritual *discernment*, not physical *senses*. But when Adam (the first man) disobeyed God, he destroyed his fellowship and communion with the Spirit of God (see Gen. 3). The consequence was death.

This death is isolation from the spirit world of God. Through disobedience, man's spirit lost contact with the Source of Heaven. As a result, man became a victim of his *soul* (mind, will, emotions) and his *body* (five senses). His life became governed by his external environment as his five senses controlled his existence.

The relationship between man and his environment gave birth to humanistic philosophy. Man started living and interpreting his existence according to the *information* he gained through the senses of his body, instead of the *revelation* received through his spirit from the Spirit of God. This change has caused man to limit his potential ability to the capabilities of his senses and his physical body.

But we have this treasure in earthen vessels, that the excellence of the power may be of God and not of us (2 Corinthians 4:7 NKJV).

The human body was specifically designed to relate to and pick up the earth or physical realm. God did not intend the body to relate to the spiritual or supernatural world. It is essential, then, that we do not judge our true potential by the abilities or limitations of our physical bodies. Because our five senses are specifically designed to "pick up" our natural environment, our powers of sight, touch, hearing, smell, and taste are all related to the natural, physical world. The potential of our bodies is therefore governed by its physical capabilities. You were not created to be intimidated by your environment.

No matter how majestic and wonderful the human body is, we must be careful to remember the reality of its composition. According to Genesis 2:7, the Manufacturer of this magnificent masterpiece made and formed it from the *"dust of the ground."* The body is 100 percent *dirt*. The apostle Paul called the spirit in human bodies "[heavenly] *treasure in earthen vessels*" (2 Cor. 4:7). We must, therefore, understand that our bodies—though they have tremendous potentials, powers, capabilities, and values—must never become the full measure of our potential.

Therefore we do not lose heart. Though outwardly we are wasting away, yet inwardly we are being renewed day by day (2 Corinthians 4:16).

There are millions of physically handicapped individuals who, because of their society's concept of potential, have resigned themselves to a life of self-pity, depression, and isolation. There are many who have confused their bodies with their true selves. They have mistaken the "house" for the "resident."

But history gives ample evidence of thousands who have freed themselves of the myth that their bodies should dictate their true potential.

Helen Keller refused to be blinded by others' opinions of her ability—she changed the attitude of the world. Sir Winston Churchill refused to be muted by his speech impediment and physical handicap—while a member of the British Parliament and later the prime minister of Britain, he delivered some of history's most life-changing orations.

What is your handicap? Is it a wheelchair, the socio-economic status of your family, the color of your skin? Are you disabled by divorce, incest, or child abuse? Whatever your *perceived* handicap, you must never allow your true potential to become a victim of the limitations of your physical body or your environment. Reach beyond your grasp. Your body is not your full potential.

As it is written: "I have made you a father of many nations." He is our father in the sight of God, in whom he believed... Against all hope, Abraham in hope believed and so became the father of many nations... Without weakening in his faith, he faced the fact that his body was as good as dead... being fully persuaded that God had power to do what He had promised (Romans 4:17-21).

D evelop and maintain a correct attitude toward your body. Learn to see it from the perspective of God, its Creator, who (through the apostle Paul) calls it "the temple of the living God" (see 2 Cor. 6:16). God admonishes you to keep your temple holy, clean, and healthy.

Therefore we do not lose heart. Though outwardly we are wasting away, yet inwardly we are being renewed day by day (2 Corinthians 4:16).

The key to Abraham's success is related to his attitude toward his body. He was handicapped by age and his wife was handicapped by a barren womb. But they considered not their bodies and believed that God had provided the potential to fulfill the demand being placed upon them. You must refuse to limit your true potential by the limitations of your physical body.

The mind of sinful man is death, but the mind controlled by the Spirit is life and peace (Romans 8:6).

Some years ago a famous pop singer sang a song entitled "I'm a Soul Man." I suspect he was referring to the cultural-ethnic orientation of the African-American artistic expression. But the statement communicates both a statement of truth and a myth. The *soul* is the triunity of the *mind*, the *will*, and the *emotions*. The soul was created for the purpose of receiving revelation from the spirit-man to communicate it to the body and *information* from the physical senses to transmit it to the spirit-man. In essence, the soul was designed to be the "*servant*" of the spirit-man, and the body was designed to be the "servant" of the soul. Man is a spirit, lives in a body, and possesses a soul. But the Fall of Man changed that.

When Adam disobeyed God's words, his spirit lost fellowship with God's Spirit and was paralyzed. Man was reduced to a "soul man." The exercise of the soul can make you smart, but not wise.

You are as potent as your Creator says you are.

And if the Spirit of Him who raised Jesus from the dead is living in you, He who raised Christ from the dead will also give life to your mortal bodies through His Spirit, who lives in you (Romans 8:11).

The measure of your true potential is your *spirit*. God has always intended that you and I would live from the inside—from the spirit-man in communion with the eternal *Spirit of God*. Paul wrote: *"The **mind** of sinful man is death, but the **mind** controlled by the Spirit is life and peace"* (Rom. 8:6, emphasis added).

The mind controlled by the Spirit is like a fountain of life gushing forth with the potential of God through the Spirit of God. Paul also writes: *"Those who live according to the sinful nature have their minds set on what that nature desires; but those who live in accordance with the **Spirit** have their minds set on what the **Spirit** desires"* (Rom. 8:5, emphasis added).

God has information on your ability and potential that will astonish you and your family.

The measure of your true potential is hidden in the Spirit of God.

*Your word is a lamp to my feet and a light
for my path* (Psalm 119:105).

We are excellent, complexly designed, tremendously built, intricately put together pieces of equipment. But we don't know what we can do. We can't even imagine the full extent of our capabilities. Through His Word, the Bible, God tells us the potential of this equipment called human beings. In His Manual, He lists all the things we are capable of doing.

When God first presented this piece of equipment called man, something went wrong. Instead of taking it back to the Manufacturer to be fixed, we took it to a second-rate, second-class, unskilled technician—satan. And he muddled the job. We submitted God's equipment and product to an unauthorized dealer with no "genuine parts."

But God loved us so much that, even though the warranty had run out, He decided to take back the product. God is starting all over—and He's putting in His own parts. God is rebuilding and remaking us because He is our Creator. His Word reveals much about His attitude toward our potential.

Without faith it is impossible to please God... (Hebrews 11:6).

G od sees you as being in His class. Because He made you in His image, you have the potential to be in the God class—which is spirit. You have the potential to operate like God.

Then God said, "Let Us make man in Our image, in Our likeness..." (Genesis 1:26).

When God made you in His likeness, He did not make you to *look* like Him. He made you to function like Him. That's what *likeness* literally means. When God created you, He made you to operate like Him.

If you are not functioning like God, you are "malfunctioning," because God wired and designed you to function like Him. How does God function? God functions by faith. You and I were designed to operate by faith.

God created you to rule over all the earth and everything that creeps in it. Thus, if the earth in any way is dominating you, you are malfunctioning. God did not intend for you to be controlled by alcohol, nicotine, drugs, sex, money, power, or greed. If any of these are governing you, you are living below your privilege. Everything in the earth must be under your subjection, not mastering you.

For the word of the Lord is right and true;
He is faithful in all He does (Psalm 33:4).

———————

Y ou have the ability to be fruitful and reproduce
after your kind (see Gen. 1:28). Again God is
calling forth something that's already in you. He did
not tell the man and the woman to *try* to be fruitful,
He simply told them to do it. He knew they already
had the ability to multiply and reproduce and fill the
earth. You too can reproduce yourself. Whatever
God calls you to do, He has already built in.

God gave you the ability to imagine and plan
and bring into being anything you desire. If you
decide to do something, and you believe in it hard
enough and commit yourself to work for it long
enough, nothing in the universe can stop you. If you
want to do anything, God already said, "You can do
it." Only if you lack the commitment to follow after
your dream will your dream remain unfinished.

The potential to do and plan anything is in you
if you will believe and persevere.

Your word, O Lord, is eternal; it stands firm in the heavens (Psalm 119:89).

You have the potential to influence physical and spiritual matter.

I will give you the keys of the kingdom of heaven; whatever you bind on earth will be bound in heaven, and whatever you loose on earth will be loosed in heaven (Matthew 16:19).

Jesus is talking here about your power to influence what's on earth as well as what's in Heaven. You have influence in Heaven. You have the power to influence things in both realms of earth and Heaven.

If you remain in Me and My words remain in you, ask whatever you wish, and it will be given you (John 15:7).

God says you have the potential to receive whatever you ask. You have a blank check—but you must abide in Christ, and His words must abide in you. If that condition is met, you can ask anything in Jesus' name and it will be done for you. But first He requires that you stay hooked up with God. Then He says, "Go ahead and ask Me for anything. I'll do whatever you ask." What potential!

*May the grace of the Lord Jesus Christ, and
the love of God, and the fellowship of the
Holy Spirit be with you all* (2 Corinthians
13:14).

S in, or rebellion against God, clogs up our potential. Disobedience to God may have stunted your
capacity for growth. But God sees and cares about that
problem. He sent Jesus into the world to die for you.

It is my earnest desire that you will realize the
awesome wealth of potential residing in you. But
more important than this potential is to understand
your need for a personal relationship with your
Creator through Jesus Christ.

I encourage you to pray the following prayer:
Dear heavenly Father, Creator, and Manufacturer of my life, today I submit my life to
You, totally surrendering the product of my
whole life to You for complete repair, maintenance, and renewal in Jesus Christ. I confess
Him as the only Savior of my life and submit to
Him as my Lord. By faith, I this moment
receive the Holy Spirit, who, by His power,
makes me an eternal citizen of Your Kingdom of
Heaven. I commit myself to serve and acknowledge You in all my ways as I endeavor to maximize my potential for Your praise and glory…
This I pray in Jesus' name, Amen.

His divine power has given us everything we need for life and godliness through our knowledge of Him who called us by His own glory and goodness (2 Peter 1:3).

Here are the first five keys to releasing your full potential.

Key #1—Know (be related to) your Source.

God guarantees the maximum performance of our potential if we submit to the conditions, specifications, and standards set by Him.

Key #2—Understand how you were designed to function.

God created and designed humankind to function like He does—by faith and love.

Key #3—Know your purpose.

Purpose gives birth to responsibility, and responsibility makes demands on potential.

Key #4—Understand your resources.

God provided for human beings tremendous material and physical resources to sustain and maintain us as we proceed in realizing, developing, and maximizing our potential.

Key #5—Have the right environment.

God created everything to flourish within a specific environment. The Fall of Man contaminated his environment and poisoned the atmosphere of our potential. The key to releasing our true potential is the restoration of God's original environment. Jesus came to restore us to the Father. He sent the Holy Spirit to restore our internal environment.

Therefore, my dear friends, as you have always obeyed—not only in my presence, but now much more in my absence—continue to work out your salvation with fear and trembling (Philippians 2:12).

Here are the remaining keys to releasing your full potential.

Key #6—Work out your potential.

Good ideas do not bring success. To release your true potential, you must be willing to work.

Key #7—Cultivate your potential.

Feed your potential the fertilizer of good positive company, give it the environment of encouragement, pour out the water of the Word of God, and bathe it in the sunshine of personal prayer.

Key #8—Guard your potential.

Guard your visions and dreams from sin, discouragement, procrastination, failures, opinions, distractions, traditions, and compromise.

Key #9—Share your potential.

True potential and fulfillment in life is not based on what is accomplished, but on who benefits. Your deposit was given to enrich and inspire others.

Key #10—Know and understand the laws of limitation.

Freedom and power are two important elements in life. Potential is the essence of both.

All of these keys and principles are proven to be true. Commit to obeying the Manufacturer. Then watch your life unfold as you discover the hidden ability that was always within you.

For everyone who has will be given more, and he will have an abundance. Whoever does not have, even what he has will be taken from him (Matthew 25:29).

The Bible tells us a story about people who decided to build a city with a tower that reached to the heavens. When God saw how committed the builders were to their task He said, *"...nothing they plan to do will be impossible for them."* So He came down and confused their languages so they couldn't work together (see Gen. 11:8).

Do you think God was against the tower? No. God was against the goal of the tower. The people did not have a relationship with God. They were ungodly men and women who intended to build a tower to Heaven so *their* names could be great. They weren't interested in making God's name great; they wanted to make a name for themselves.

Humankind has accomplished many things without God. Imagine what would happen if they were hooked up with God. Jesus came to provide that hookup.

If you have accepted Jesus as your Lord and Savior, I'm here to encourage you to move on with the real things of God. What have you done since you were saved? What have you accomplished?

Therefore do not worry about tomorrow, for tomorrow will worry about itself. Each day has enough trouble of its own (Matthew 6:34).

———————

Maslow, one of the greatest influences on the thought patterns of psychology in our world, theorized that human beings are driven by their base needs. He believed that our most immediate need becomes our controlling factor—shelter, food, security, or protection. As each need is met, then we begin to move up the ladder until we focus on becoming self-realized and self-actualized, etc. According to this theory, we are ruled by our base needs.

In Matthew chapter 6, Jesus challenges that theory. He instructs us to live from the perspective of what we cannot see, rather than being caught up in the needs of our daily lives. God lives and thinks in the potential. Jesus simply asks us to have faith—to believe in God's goodness and care.

According to God, Maslow was wrong—and I go with God. There are people who have everything, but they still don't know who they are. Ask the guy at the top who can't sleep. Ask the woman who has everything except peace and love and joy in her heart. Maslow was wrong. God desires to give you self-worth and self-esteem first. He wants you to know who you are *first*.

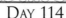
But seek first His kingdom and His righteousness, and all these things will be given to you as well (Matthew 6:33).

I have met so many people who have everything except the knowledge of who they are. Jesus said, "Why worry about these things? Life is so much more than these things about which you worry. Life is peace and love and joy and patience and gentleness…"

Seek first the things of God and everything else you need will just fall into place. The mind controlled by the Spirit of God is full of life and peace. Peace is so important to a fulfilled life. It goes hand in hand with the life Jesus came to bring. You don't have to worry when you know what is coming. When you live by the Spirit in the realm of the unseen and the invisible, there is no reason to worry. God is holding what is in store for you, because all things that are, were, and will be are in God.

When we are distracted by our drive for personal security and our search for identity, we rarely achieve our true potential. We are so caught up trying to make it *through* life that we don't have time to be *in* life.

*Therefore I say unto you, What things so-ever ye **desire**, when ye pray, believe that ye receive them, and ye shall have them* (Mark 11:24 KJV, emphasis added).

———◆———

Very often the Church has misread the word *desire*. We have expected, perhaps, that the word *desire* means "what we are dreaming about." No. *Desire* is "craving enough to sacrifice for." Only if we are willing to die for what we desire will we receive it.

God is pregnant with everything that isn't yet visible—including what you ask for in prayer.

When you ask for something in faith, it is already on the way. You can't see it, but if you believe, it is already in process. Thus, whatever you desire when you pray, you shall have—*but only what you desire*. Not what you *pray* for—only what you *desire when you pray*.

This life is full of advertisements for your attention. If you don't have a goal, they will provide one for you. You must know where you want to go and what you want to become.

When you pray, desire what you ask for. Refuse to be distracted or interrupted. The power of your potential will be revealed as you sacrifice everything to attain what you desired in prayer.

Enter through the narrow gate. For wide is the gate and broad is the road that leads to destruction, and many enter through it. But small is the gate and narrow the road that leads to life, and only a few find it (Matthew 7:13-14).

These words have saved my sanity. I want all who read these words to fulfill their potential; but I know only a few will. Only a minute percentage of those who hear the message about who they are will ever become all they could be. Many people will never fulfill their purpose in life. They will not be who they were supposed to be or achieve what they were designed to do.

It's terrible to say, but that's why I'm sharing this with you. If only I could take my desire and put it into you, I'd do it. But I can't. Some of you will end up in the gutter because you won't receive and practice what God is telling you. I'm sorry, but it will happen. Whether you fail or succeed, win or lose, does not depend on God, but on you. He is ready to do His part if you are willing to cooperate with His purpose for your life.

As a prisoner for the Lord, then, I urge you to live a life worthy of the calling you have received (Ephesians 4:1).

Your Creator and Manufacturer built a store of miracles in you. He said you have treasures in your earthen vessel. He came to bring you abundant life. He knows there is explosive power in you waiting to be released. Through the strength of Jesus Christ you can do anything you think or imagine—and even more. But not everyone will hook up with God. Not everyone will look for the things God planted within them to be used for His glory. Not everyone will choose to fulfill their potential. Indeed, the number will be few.

Will you dare to believe the impossible no matter what others say? The world needs people who will believe God for the potential buried within them—desiring their dreams enough to move out and act. Only a few will find the kind of potential that allows them to live from the depths of their hidden ability. But for those who do, deep wells of possibilities will come to light as God reveals to them more and more of what He planned before the foundations of the world.

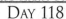

For though we live in the world, we do not wage war as the world does (2 Corinthians 10:3).

Today there are over 5 billion people on planet Earth. Over half of these people live in countries and conditions that have been labeled *Third World*. This term was invented by a French economist to describe groupings of peoples throughout the world based on socio-economic status.

I was born and live in a part of the world that is said to fall within this category. The term is defined as any people who did not benefit from or participate in the industrial revolution. Many of them were reduced to slaves and indentured servants, thus robbing them of their identity, dignity, self-worth, and self-respect.

It is crucial that we do not inhibit our potential to chart a new course for the future by being destroyed by our preoccupation with the past. We have the responsibility to deposit the wealth of our potential in this generation so the next generation can build their future on our faithfulness to becoming everything we can possibly be.

*But I have raised you up for this very pur-
pose, that I might show you My power and
that My name might be proclaimed in all
the earth* (Exodus 9:16).

———————

The poorest person in the world is the person
without a dream. The most frustrated person in
the world is the person with a dream that never
becomes reality. I am certain that every individual
on this planet—no matter which race, culture,
nationality, or socio-economic status—has had a
dream of some sort.

The ability of children to dream is a natural
instinct instilled by the Creator. I am convinced that
God created and gave us the gift of imagination to
provide us with a glimpse of our purpose in life and
to activate the hidden ability within each of us. Your
purpose is the source of the dream and the vision
you carried in your heart from childhood. It is the
key to your fulfillment.

In Exodus 9, we see that Pharaoh, one of earth's
most powerful rulers, was in spiritual poverty
because he lacked God's dream. Yet, even Pharaoh
was raised up for God's purposes. How much more
are we a part of God's plan and Kingdom purpose?
We just need to dream a little.

For where your treasure is, there your heart will be also (Matthew 6:21).

⎯•⎯•⎯

The purpose of a tree seed is to reproduce trees. Therefore, by God's design, tree seeds possess the ability or potential to fulfill this purpose. But just because a seed has the *potential* to produce a forest, does not mean it will. One of the greatest tragedies in nature is the destruction of a seed or the isolation of a seed from the soil. Consequently, the death of a seed is the burial of a forest. Having ability is good, but keeping ability is bad.

Your life has the potential to fulfill your purpose. If, however, you imprison that potential, you rob your life of its purpose and fulfillment. You and every other individual on this planet possess an awesome treasure. Too much of this treasure is buried every day, untapped and untouched, in the cemeteries of our world. Much talent, skill, and creativity have been lost to the world for want of a little courage. Many obscure men and women enter eternity pregnant with potential, with a still-born purpose. Dying with ability reveals irresponsibility. Living with ability brings responsibility.

Guard the good deposit that was entrusted to you—guard it with the help of the Holy Spirit who lives in us (2 Timothy 1:14).

Everything in creation was designed to function on the simple principle of receiving and releasing. Life depends on this principle. What if the plants refused to release the oxygen they possess, or if we human beings refused to release the carbon dioxide we produce? The result would be chaos and death for the entire planet.

Dormant potential is not healthy, advantageous, safe, or effective. Your valuable deposit of potential was given to enrich the lives of others. When potential is kept, it self-destructs.

We have a responsibility to use what God stored in us for the good of the world. Many of us are aware of the ability we have inside, but we have been frustrated by our failure to release that ability. Some of us blame our historical circumstances. Others blame social status. Still others transfer the responsibility for their failure and frustration to their lack of formal education or their less than ideal opportunities.

You must not add to the wealth of the graveyard. You owe it to the next generation to live courageously so the treasure of your potential is unleashed.

I cry out to God Most High, to God, who fulfills His purpose for me (Psalm 57:2).

It was a cool, wet, rainy September Sunday afternoon in the historic city of London. I took the opportunity to steal away for a private, relaxing walk. After I had walked for a few minutes, the pathway meandered to the entrance of an old cemetery. I came upon a small grave, perhaps three feet in length, that read, "Markus Rogers, 1906-1910." Written below the name was the quote, "Gone but not forgotten."

After scanning the hundreds of markers and stones, my eyes rested, once again, upon the grave of this child. I noticed that almost all the tombstones, including the child's, had the words "Rest in Peace" inscribed on them.

Many questions and thoughts raced through my mind: *What was the cause of death? What was his purpose in being born? What special natural talents and gifts did he possess that were never displayed and never benefited anyone? What inventions or discoveries could he have shared with the human race? How many great works of art, books, or songs died in this precious infant?*

The world needs what God deposited in you for the benefit of your contemporaries and all the generations to follow.

If you, then, though you are evil, know how to give good gifts to your children, how much more will your Father in Heaven give good gifts to those who ask Him! (Matthew 7:11)

When in that London cemetery, I wondered: *How can you rest in peace if you died with all your potential inside?* As the wet, misty rain formed dew drops on my cheeks, I walked away thinking: *What a tragedy it is for a child to die at a tender age, before he has the opportunity to realize his full potential.*

Immediately a quiet voice screamed in my head: *Is it not a greater tragedy if those who lived to old age also carried their books, art, music, inventions, dreams, and potential to the grave?* Suddenly, the rain seemed to turn to sweat as I pondered the awesome implications of this question. I trust that you will not allow the grave to rob this world of your latent, awesome *potential*.

Deep within you lies a seed of greatness waiting to be germinated. You have been endued with natural talents, gifts, desires, and dreams. All humanity, in all cultures, races, and socio-economic situations, lives with the natural instinct to manifest this potential.

You did not choose me, but I chose you and appointed you to go and bear fruit—fruit that will last. Then the Father will give you whatever you ask in My name (John 15:16).

The entire creation possesses this principle of potential. Everything has the natural instinct to release its ability. The Bible states that God created everything with *"seed in it according to their kinds"* (Gen. 1:12). In essence, hidden within everything is the potential to fulfill itself and produce much more than we see.

When God created the earth and placed man in the Garden, He did not give man a finished product. Although God knew that man would need food, clothes, shelter, transportation, and other elements of comfort, He did not make all these things instantly available.

Henry Ford said, "My best friend is the one who brings out the best in me." It is my hope that this book becomes one of your best friends as it inspires you to strive to release your hidden abilities for the benefit of the world around you and for your personal fulfillment.

The releasing of your potential is not up to God but you.

And we, who with unveiled faces all reflect the Lord's glory, are being transformed into His likeness with ever-increasing glory, which comes from the Lord, who is the Spirit (2 Corinthians 3:18).

For the last two decades, I have devoted myself to understanding, activating, tapping, and releasing my potential and the potential of others. An integral part of this devotion was the study of the lives of people who have affected their societies positively because they released and maximized their potential. As a result, I am convinced that every individual comes into this world with a deposit of potential that far exceeds any attempt to measure its potency.

I believe, with great sadness, that not everyone will become all the Creator intended. Too many people are mere products of their environments—victims of others' opinions and the assessments of human analysis. They lack the will to change or challenge the limitations placed upon them by themselves and others, and fail to take the necessary steps to develop their potential.

I also believe, however, that anyone, of any age, and in any circumstances, can transform himself or herself if he or she wants to. It's not what you don't know that hurts you. It's what you know that just ain't so.

Therefore, since we are surrounded by such a great cloud of witnesses, let us throw off everything that hinders and the sin that so easily entangles, and let us run with perseverance the race marked out for us (Hebrews 12:1).

———◆———

It was my first trip to Brazil where I would be addressing a conference of 10,000 leaders and laymen. I felt an awesome responsibility upon me.

Seven days into my stay, my host and translator took me on a tour of the capital city, Brasilia. We visited government buildings and toured the stately monuments, and we visited one of my favorite places—the national museum.

As I admired the historical pieces, I was once again reminded that each painting, sculpture, and specimen was the product of the release of someone's potential. Because they had dared to expose the talent hidden within them, I and many others were enjoying, appreciating, and being inspired by their imaginative works.

Throughout time, the great and small works of individuals have affected the lives of many. All who have helped to shape our society's destiny used their potential with a passion and refused to let circumstances dictate their future. *Their released potential is the world's inheritance.*

Whether you are seeking to impact 10,000 lives or one life, your efforts will affect many.

Nothing in all creation is hidden from God's sight. Everything is uncovered and laid bare before the eyes of Him to whom we must give account (Hebrews 4:13).

I believe earth itself is a museum. Each of us comes into this world with an assignment to fulfill. God commissions us to leave for the following generations something from which they can learn and be inspired. The abilities to complete these assignments lie within us.

The tools are our natural talents, gifts, and ambitions.

Throughout time, the great and small works of individuals—be they paintings, books, music, poetry, drama, architecture, inventions, or the development of theories—have affected the lives of many. All who have helped to shape our society's destiny— the giants who teach us and inspire us—used their potential with a passion and refused to allow circumstances to dictate their future. Museums are a constant reminder that someone lived who refused to let death have the final word on their potential.

Accept the responsibility for activating your abilities, so the next generation will not enter the museum of life and notice a vacant space in earth's displays.

So he called him in and asked him, "What is this I hear about you? Give an account of your management, because you cannot be manager any longer" (Luke 16:2).

———•———

"The price of greatness is responsibility." These words were spoken by Sir Winston Churchill.

Abortion is one of today's most controversial issues. It is polarizing many communities. It has also become a hot political issue in many countries where it is used to manipulate the reins of power. Many people think of this concern as a recent one. Although it is causing much stir in our societies, the concern over abortion is not new. The truth is that the abortion issue is as old as time. The fact of abortion is as old as man.

Abortion is not limited to the physical termination of a fetus in a mother's womb. The first act of abortion was performed in the Garden of Eden when the first man, Adam, was given the responsibility of carrying the entire human race within his loins. In Adam was the seed of all generations and the strength of all humankind.

To abort means to terminate life before its full potential has or can be realized, before the person is given an opportunity to fulfill its full potential.

But I tell you that men will have to give account on the day of judgment for every careless word they have spoken (Matthew 12:36).

God created everything with the hidden ability to fulfill itself. The Bible's record of creation states that the seed of everything is in itself to produce after its kind (see Gen. 1:12). All creation possesses the hidden ability to be everything it is suppose to be.

It is important to remember that every great tree was once a seed, every woman was once a fetus, every man was once a child, and every nation was once in the loins of a man. It is also interesting to note that *whenever God deals with man, He always speaks in terms of the generational seed within his loins*. In God's calculation of life, one equals many, little equals much, small equals great, and less equals more. Therefore, to abort a seed is to kill a forest, to abort a cow is to kill a herd, to abort a boy is to kill a man, to abort a girl is to kill a woman, and to abort a person is to destroy a nation.

Abortion is the ultimate tragedy. It robs life of its essence and denies the future its value.

So then, each of us will give an account of himself to God (Romans 14:12).

A bortion is the ignorance of responsibility and the denial of obligation. Abortion is self-comfort at the expense of fruitfulness, because *all abortions sacrifice responsibility*. The abortion of potential condemns the future. This reality has caused the development of an entire discipline of science. Ecology and environmental studies, as these areas of concern are known, build their premises on the word *extinction*, meaning "the termination of the potential force within creation to fulfill itself."

It is amazing that man, with all his attempts to minimize the abortion of various species in the animal and plant kingdom by investing billions of dollars to protect animals, plants, forests, and the ozone layer, has neglected to prioritize the position of human beings in the scheme of things. While people fight to protect whales, owls, trees, and fish, they also battle for the right to terminate human babies. Perhaps the situation would improve if every doctor who performs this tragic operation would be reminded before each abortion that the opportunity to perform this surgery is his (or hers) only because his mother did not abort him.

For all have sinned and fall short of the glory of God (Romans 3:23).

———◆———

*T*he abortion of potential is the death of the future. It affects generation after generation. When Adam broke God's law, he aborted his seed's potential for becoming all they were intended to be. Men and women throughout all ages have fallen far short of the glory of the Creator. The word glory means the "true nature" or "full essence" of a thing. In other words, *to fall short of glory means to live below your true potential*. This is what God calls sin. Sin is not a behavior; it is a disposition. Apostle Paul writes:

> *I consider that our present sufferings are not worth comparing with the glory that will be revealed in us. The creation waits in eager expectation for* [the glory of] *the sons of God to be revealed* (Romans 8:18-19).

This passage states that the Fall of Man prevented the full glory or true potential of humankind from being revealed or manifested. Thus, any abortion, whether it's the abortion of a dream, a vision, art, music, writing, business, leadership, or inventions, affects both nature and the succeeding generations. *How many children yet unborn are destined to sing the song you have yet to write?*

But the gift is not like the trespass. For if the many died by the trespass of the one man, how much more did God's grace and the gift that came by the grace of the one man, Jesus Christ, overflow to the many! (Romans 5:15)

When Adam aborted the vision God had placed in his heart and disobeyed the directives of the Manufacturer, he changed the lives of the entire human race that lay hidden in his loins.

If your potential is not released, it will affect this generation and all the generations yet to live. Even creation will testify against you. If you abort your potential, you will be guilty of robbing the world of the treasure you came to this planet to deliver.

The fact that you were born is evidence that God knew earth needed the potential you are pregnant with. It is, therefore, imperative that you refuse to leave this planet without giving birth to those dreams, ideas, visions, and inventions you carry in the womb of your faith right now. Do not abort your baby of potential. *Rob the grave of the treasure you carry.* Leave the picture of your potential on the wall of history in the museum of the earth.

For acquiring a disciplined and prudent life, doing what is right and just and fair (Proverbs 1:3).

———◆———

Come with me in your imagination to the funeral of a loved one. Picture yourself driving to the funeral parlor or the church, parking your car, and getting out. As you walk inside the building, you feel the shared sorrow of losing and the joy of having known that radiates from the hearts of the people there.

As you walk to the front of the room and look inside the casket, you come face to face with yourself. This is your funeral, five years from today. All these people have come to honor you and to express feelings of love and appreciation for your life. As you look at the program in your hand, you see that the first speaker is from your family. The second speaker is a friend. The third is from your work or profession. The fourth speaker is from your church or some community organization where you were involved in service. The fifth and final speaker is your spouse.

Now think deeply. What would you like each of these speakers to say about you and your life?

For who knows what is good for a man in life, during the few and meaningless days he passes through like a shadow? Who can tell him what will happen under the sun after he is gone? (Ecclesiastes 6:12)

I am trying to help you become aware of the great treasure you possess, which is your potential. I have addressed millions of people on this issue of living effectively. Repeatedly I have stressed that it is better to have never been born than to live and not fulfill the purpose for which you were given life. This truth is echoed in Ecclesiastes 6:3-5:

A man may have a hundred children and live many years; yet no matter how long he lives, if he cannot enjoy his prosperity and does not receive proper burial, I say that a stillborn child is better off than he. It comes without meaning, it departs in darkness, and in darkness its name is shrouded. Though it never saw the sun or knew anything, it has more rest than does that man.

In essence, when you become aware of the tremendous potential that resides within you, you are obligated to release that wealth to the world around you.

Brothers, each man, as responsible to God, should remain in the situation God called him to (1 Corinthians 7:24).

———◆———

"What lies behind you and what lies in front of you, pales in comparison to what lies inside of you," as Ralph Waldo Emerson said.

You may not be able to change your past, and your future is yet unlived, but the present provides you with opportunities to maximize your life and the ability that lives within you. You must take responsibility for your ability—no one else can do it for you.

Are you living a stillborn life? Are you aborting your entire purpose for living? I encourage you to take responsibility right now for your ability. Determine to activate, release, and maximize your potential for the sake of the next generation. Leave your footprints in the sands of the history of your country. *Live fully so you can die effectively. Let your life write the speech of your death and give your potential to humankind for the glory of God.*

Remember "well done" is much better than "well said." Don't just talk about your potential dreams, visions, and ideas. Step out now and determine to do them.

May the favor of the Lord our God rest upon us; establish the work of our hands for us—yes, establish the work of our hands (Psalm 90:17).

Because potential, by definition, is the large, unknown bank of resources you were given at birth, what you have accomplished is no longer your potential. Releasing your potential requires a willingness to move beyond the familiar into the realm of possibilities.

If you attempt new things and make choices that stretch your horizons, you will embark on an exciting journey. You will begin to see the marvelous being God created you to be—a being filled with more capabilities than you ever dreamed possible. The journey begins when you gain an understanding of what potential is and how you can release it. Once you understand the magnitude of the wealth God gave you, to then turn away from consciously and conscientiously unwrapping God's gift is to abort your potential and refuse to fulfill the purpose for which He gave you life.

Potential is given to be released, not wasted. Some people have thousands of reasons why they cannot do what they want to, when all they need is one reason why they can.

*For you have been born again, not of per-
ishable seed, but of imperishable, through
the living and enduring Word of God* (1 Peter
1:23).

Potential is the sum of who you are that you have
yet to reveal. Unless you continually try to reach
higher, go farther, see over, and grasp something
greater than you now know, you will never discover
your full potential.

If, for example, I hold an apple seed in my hand,
in truth I hold an entire orchard. That is potential—
what yet can be.

God created everything with potential. Genesis
1:12 describes how God created the plants and the
trees, each *"bearing seed according to their kinds."*
Each possessed the capability to be much more than
they appeared to be at any one time. Each contained
the seed from which future generations of plants,
birds, fish, and animals would come.

Like the apple seed, you possess hidden resources
and capabilities. Most of the potential God gave you
at birth still remains within you, unseen and unused.
What I see when I meet you on any given day is not
all you are. God planted within you the ability to be
much more than you are at any one moment.

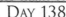
I am the Alpha and the Omega, the First and the Last, the Beginning and the End (Revelation 22:13).

Everything that was and is was in God. Before God created anything, there was only God. Thus, God had within Him the potential for everything He made. Nothing exists that was not first in God. Indeed, the beginning was in God before it began. God started start. If the Book of Genesis had started with Genesis 1:0, it might have read, *"Before there was a beginning, there was God. Before there was a creation, there was a Creator. Before anything was, there was God."*

God did not begin when the beginning began. He was in the beginning before the beginning had a beginning. *"In the beginning was the Word, and the Word was with God, and the Word was God"* (John 1:1). Everything in the world we know was in God before it came to be seen. *"Through [God] all things were made; without Him nothing was made that has been made"* (John 1:3). Thus, God is the source of all potential. He is everything we haven't seen yet.

My flesh and my heart may fail, but God is the strength of my heart and my portion forever (Psalm 73:26).

God's process in creating the world follows an interesting pattern. *First, God planned what He wanted to create. Second, He decided what kind of material substance He wanted His creation to be made from. Third, God spoke to the substance from which the thing was to be created and, fourth, exactly what He spoke came forth from that to which He spoke.*

You came forth from God because God planned that human beings should be spirit even as He is Spirit. Too many people never discover God's purpose for creating them. They look everywhere but to God for the meaning of their existence. Their lives are unfulfilled and their potential is wasted. God looks at them and bemoans their loss: "If you only knew who you are. If you only knew what you can do. If you only knew why I gave you life."

Remember, few things are impossible when they are tackled with diligence and skill. Great works are performed not by strength, but by perseverance. God created you with potential. He waits to see what you will do with the remarkable gift He gave you.

How many are your works, O Lord! In wisdom you made them all; the earth is full of Your creatures (Psalm 104:24).

Before you can begin to grasp the nature and the magnitude of your potential, you must understand the laws that control all potential. The first two chapters of the Bible tell the story of this unleashing of God's potential.

The following six basic principles are fundamental to *all* potential. Here are the first two:

Principle #1—What God speaks to is the source for what He creates.

An examination of the process God used to create the world reveals that everything God created was brought forth by His spoken word. Throughout creation, whatever God spoke to became the source from which the created thing came, and exactly what God spoke came forth from the substance to which He spoke.

Principle #2—All things have the same components and essence as the sources from which they came.

The source to which God spoke during the creative process also becomes the final home of all He has created. When God's creations die, they return to the source from which He took them.

It is I who made the earth and created mankind upon it. My own hands stretched out the heavens; I marshaled their starry hosts (Isaiah 45:12).

H ere are the next two of the six principles:

Principle #3—All things must be maintained by the source from which they came.

God's world also reveals that whatever God creates must be sustained and maintained by the source from which it came. None of God's living creations can survive without the resources and the nourishment provided by the substances from which they came.

Principle #4—The potential of all things is related to the source from which they came.

Because all things are composed of the sources from which they came, they also contain as little or as much potential as their original substances.

Thus, the quality of any product is dependent upon the quality of the components used in the product, which is dependent upon the quality of the materials used in the components. *The potential of something is always related to the potential of the source from which it came.* Nothing can be greater than its source.

Have we not all one Father? Did not one God create us? (Malachi 2:10a)

H ere are the last two of the six principles:

Principle #5—Everything in life has the potential to fulfill its purpose.

The purpose of a thing is the original intent or desire of the one who created it. Thus, the purpose of a thing cannot be known by asking anyone other than the designer or the manufacturer. The manufacturer determines both the product's purpose and how it will function to fulfill that purpose.

Principle #6—The potential of something is determined and revealed by the demands placed on it by its creator.

What a product can potentially do is determined by what the manufacturer of the product asks it to do. Potential is revealed by the faith of the manufacturer in his product and the expectations he places upon it. If a manufacturer requires a product to do something, you can be sure that he believes the ability to perform the task was built into the product.

So that you may become blameless and pure, children of God without fault in a crooked and depraved generation, in which you shine like stars in the universe (Philippians 2:15).

I want to share four keys used by wise gardeners to encourage the growth of their gardens. These same principles can help you grow to maturity as you liberate all the potential that God deposited in you.

Key #1—Cultivate your potential.

Experienced gardeners know that weeds often grow faster than vegetables. If a gardener goes away for several weeks, he (or she) will return to stunted and sickly vegetable plants that yield little or no fruit. Or even worse, he may find that he has no vegetable plants at all because the weeds smothered and choked the tender shoots. Cultivation is necessary for a healthy and productive garden.

The same is true of your potential. Seek those persons who are positive and encouraging. Remove yourself from those activities and situations that might encourage you to return to your former way of life. Cling to your Source and allow Him to cleanse you of those things that would deter you from maximizing your potential. *Much emerging potential dies for want of cultivation.* The careful and consistent nurturing of your potential will enable you to meet the full responsibilities that God planned for your life.

Be self-controlled and alert. Your enemy the devil prowls around like a roaring lion looking for someone to devour (1 Peter 5:8).

Many times we are initially excited by the glimpses God gives us of the potential He planted within us. After we invite Jesus into our hearts, we may spend time in worship, prayer, and Bible study. We may look beyond our present circumstances to the unseen world of faith; we may seek God's guidance in our daily decisions as we open ourselves to His plans and purposes for our lives; and we may appreciate and treasure the many blessings He showers upon us. But as time passes, the garden of our potential tends to lose its early vitality as we allow circumstances and responsibilities to crowd and choke the imaginations and the possibilities that lie hidden within us.

Key #2—Guard your potential.

Most gardeners have experienced the frustration and the disappointment that occur when rabbits, insects, or birds destroy their carefully cultivated plants.

Satan is intent on destroying your potential. He is constantly trying to devour your abilities. The release of your full potential is directly dependent on your diligence in protecting your dreams, plans, and imaginations from the many negative influences that would block their effective fulfillment.

I planted the seed, Apollos watered it, but God made it grow. So neither he who plants nor he who waters is anything, but only God, who makes things grow. The man who plants and the man who waters have one purpose, and each will be rewarded according to his own labor (1 Corinthians 3:6-8).

K ey #3—Share your potential.

Gardening is a shared effort. While the gardener tills the ground, plants the seeds, and pulls the weeds, the plants will not bear fruit unless the bees pollinate the blossoms, the sun warms the earth, and the rain enables the soil to release its nutrients.

Maximizing your potential and the potential of the billions of people on earth is also a shared effort. *Potential is given for the benefit of many, not for the benefit of one.* There's not much gratification in writing a symphony if no musicians will share their talents to play the music.

God made human beings to live in fellowship with Himself and other human beings. A loveless life that keeps all its accomplishments to itself will soon lose the inspiration for releasing its potential. If you give freely of your gifts, aspirations, and abilities, your potential will be magnified and maximized.

What then? Shall we sin because we are not under law but under grace? By no means! Don't you know that when you offer your-selves to someone to obey him as slaves, you are slaves to the one whom you obey— whether you are slaves to sin, which leads to death, or to obedience, which leads to righteousness? But thanks be to God that, though you used to be slaves to sin, you wholeheartedly obeyed the form of teach-ing to which you were entrusted. You have been set free from sin and have become slaves to righteousness (Romans 6:15-18).

K ey #4—Know and understand the laws of limitation.

Every experienced gardener knows that there are numerous laws that affect the success or failure of a garden. While the gardener is free to ignore those laws, he does not have the power to remove the consequences of his actions.

The same is true for your potential. God has given you the freedom and the power to maximize your potential. He has established laws and com-mandments to protect your potential, and He has given you the freedom to choose either to obey or disobey them.

Oh, the depth of the riches of the wisdom and knowledge of God! How unsearchable His judgments, and His paths beyond tracing out! (Romans 11:33)

In the great depth of God's wisdom and knowledge, He has carved a path for your potential.

Everything in creation was designed to function on the simple principle of receiving and releasing. Life depends on this principle.

Building potential into a product does not necessarily mean that potential will be revealed. Many of us have appliances in our homes that are capable of much more than we require of them. Perhaps you use your oven to bake but not broil. Or maybe you have a vacuum cleaner that has the ability to clean up water as well as dirt, but you haven't used that feature.

God has built many abilities into men and women. Too often, however, we fail to use that potential because we don't understand either the magnitude of our capabilities or the requirements that are necessary to unleash our power. In the following days, I will outline the keys to the effective release of the wealth of your potential.

In this way they will lay up treasure for themselves as a firm foundation for the coming age, so that they may take hold of the life that is truly life (1 Timothy 6:19).

Your potential needs to be released or it will remain dormant within you. There are six keys to releasing your potential.

Key #1—*You must know your Source.*

Every product you purchase includes a certain degree of guarantee based on a relationship with the one from whom you bought the product. Thus, if you want to buy a car, you will first research the integrity of the various car manufacturers and the quality of their cars. Then you will look for an authorized dealer in your area who will explain and follow the manufacturer's specifications.

Know that the Lord is God. It is He who made us, and we are His; we are His people, the sheep of His pasture (Psalm 100:3).

God is your Manufacturer. If you want to know your potential, you must go to Him. Knowing God is the foundational key upon which all the other keys rest.

Your statutes are my delight; they are my counselors (Psalm 119:24).

Potential is only as good as it is released into this world. There are six keys to releasing our potential. The first key from yesterday was: You must know your Source.

Key #2—*You must understand how you were designed to function.*

Every manufacturer designs his product with certain features and specifications. Then he gives you an instruction book that clarifies the definitions of the features so you can become familiar with both the parts of the equipment and their functions. Thus, a car manufacturer describes in the manual how the engine, the brakes, the windshield wipers, etc., are supposed to operate, because he knows that you will not get optimum performance from the car unless you understand how the various parts of the car were intended to work.

God designed you with intricate features and capabilities. If you fail to learn from God how you were designed to function, you are on your way to short-circuiting. You will never release your potential unless you learn to function by faith according to God's specifications.

And we know that in all things God works for the good of those who love Him, who have been called according to His purpose (Romans 8:28).

There are six keys to releasing our potential. Today we will focus on Key #3.

Key #3—*You must know your purpose.*

When a manufacturer proposes a new product, he first clarifies the purpose of that product. Then he designs the features to accomplish his intent. Therefore, a car manufacturer will first decide whether the vehicle is to be a race car, a delivery van, or a family car. Once the vehicle's purpose has been established, the engineer will incorporate various features to meet that purpose.

Before you were born, God had a plan and a purpose for your life. Then, in accordance with that plan, He gave you special abilities and aptitudes to enable you to accomplish everything that He intended. If you are going to release your potential, you must first discover God's plan for your life. Knowing and living within God's purpose is the difference between using and abusing the gifts and capabilities God built into you.

Praise the Lord, O my soul, and forget not all His benefits (Psalm 103:2).

K ey #1—You must know your Source.

Key #2—You must understand how you were designed to function.

Key #3—You must know your purpose.

Key #4—*You must understand your resources.*

Manufacturers determine the resources that are necessary for a product to perform correctly and efficiently. A car manufacturer might specify the octane of the gasoline to be used, the pressure of the air in the tires, or the weight of the oil for the engine.

God's pattern for your life also includes specifications for the spiritual, physical, material, and soul resources that are necessary for you to live a fulfilling and productive life. Until you learn what resources God has arranged for you to enjoy, and what benefits He planned for you to receive from each resource, your potential will be stunted and your performance will be less than it could be.

So that you may be able to discern what is best and may be pure and blameless until the day of Christ (Philippians 1:10).

There are six keys to releasing our potential. Today we will focus on Key #5.

Key #5—*You must have the right environment.* Product engineers consider carefully both the ideal environment under which a product should operate and any unfavorable conditions that might influence the product's performance. While a car manufacturer might establish the ideal conditions as a sunny day with temperatures between 32 and 70 degrees, the engineer must also plan for rainy days, fog, new moon nights, and freezing or sweltering temperatures.

When God created human beings, He placed them in the Garden of Eden, where ideal conditions for their growth and fulfillment were present. When sin entered the world through Adam and Eve's disobedience, man's environment became polluted. But most men and women are not aware of the nature or the proliferation of the pollutants that have invaded their environment. The release of your potential requires both a knowledge of the specifications of the ideal environment God provided in the Garden of Eden, and a willingness to make the necessary changes to conform your surroundings to God's specifications.

The wisdom of the prudent is to give thought to their ways, but the folly of fools is deception (Proverbs 14:8).

Today we will focus on Key #6, the last key to releasing your potential. But remember the first five keys in order to guide today's study.

Key #1—You must know your Source.

Key #2—You must understand how you were designed to function.

Key #3—You must know your purpose.

Key #4—You must understand your resources.

Key #5—You must have the right environment

Key #6—*You must work out your potential.*

Most products do not achieve their purpose just by virtue of their existence. A car, for example, must transport its occupants and cargo from point A to point B. Thus, its purpose cannot be fulfilled by sitting in the driveway.

God placed Adam in an ideal environment where all the necessary resources for a productive and satisfying life were available to him. But Adam's potential would have remained locked inside him if God had not given him a job to do. Only through work was Adam's potential to name the animals revealed.

The same is true for you. Your potential will not be released until you take your thoughts, plans, and imaginations and put them into action. You must work to mine your hidden potential.

[God's] divine power has given us everything we need for life and godliness through our knowledge of Him who called us by His own glory and goodness. Through these He has given us His very great and precious promises, so that through them you may participate in the divine nature and escape the corruption in the world caused by evil desires (2 Peter 1:3-4).

When you became a Christian, God changed your name. He said, "I know you aren't acting like My child, but you are My child. The mess you're in is just a temporary condition. Now that your spirit and My Spirit are reconnected, I can work in you so that your behavior can catch up with your nature. Who you've been is not who you are."

You are supposed to be naturally like your Source. God's commands do not require you to live supernaturally, but naturally. If you are a Christian, your natural mode of operation is the same as God's because you came out of Him, and the product always has the nature of its source. God expects you to act and think like He does because He is your Source/Creator and you are His child.

Jesus gave them this answer: "I tell you the truth, the Son can do nothing by Himself; He can do only what He sees His Father doing, because whatever the Father does the Son also does" (John 5:19).

What you can do is related to where you came from. God is serious when He says, "Without Me you can do nothing." It's not a matter of being spiritual, it just plain business sense. He created and made you. You came from Him. Therefore, the quality of your abilities is defined by God's abilities. You share God's potential to plan, design, and bring dreams into reality. God is full of more projects, ambitions, and proposals than you can imagine. He's the God of the impossible. But He has tied the revelation of His potential to your dreams, aspirations, and prayers. That's why God is constantly challenging you to ask Him for the impossible. The possible is no fun for God. He's already done that. It's the ideas, plans, and objectives the world hasn't seen yet that God wants to do.

You are the key to God's creative expression.

To one he gave five talents of money, to another two talents, and to another one talent, each according to his ability (Matthew 25:15a).

You will never know your purpose unless you figure out why God created you. Only God can tell you your purpose, because He determined it when He gave you life.

The direction you need to live a satisfying and rewarding life cannot be found in your family, your teachers, your employer, your pastor, or your coworkers. They are creatures even as you are. *The only way you can discover your purpose is through a relationship with the One who made you.*

God has determined the resources you need to live a happy, productive life, because He is the only One who knows what you need to meet the demands He will place upon you. If you are constantly comparing your resources with those of other people, you will be blinded to the richness of what God has entrusted to you. The release of your full potential demands that you examine your life carefully so you can identify both the many assets God has given you and the purpose for which He gave them.

God will not entrust you with more resources until you use wisely what He's already given you.

The Lord brought me forth as the first of His works, before His deeds of old; I was appointed from eternity, from the beginning, before the world began (Proverbs 8:22-23).

Your Creator/Source is the only One who is qualified to define your optimal environment. He does so through His laws and commandments. God's laws establish the elements of your ideal environment and set the necessary requirements for consistent, healthy growth. *God's commandments help you to maintain your environment.* They serve as indicators of the state of your health and the condition of your environment. Your well-being is dependent upon your understanding of God's laws and your obedience to His commandments. You can't afford to break God's commandments because disobedience brings a polluted environment, which stunts and impedes the release of your potential.

You have the potential to perform great exploits for God. But if you fail to maintain the environment God decrees, nothing will happen in your life. It doesn't matter how much you brag about what you can do or what you would like to do, or how much you can see and dream and imagine; if God's requirements aren't met, you aren't going to expose your true self!

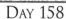

For this reason, since the day we heard about you, we have not stopped praying for you and asking God to fill you with the knowledge of His will through all spiritual wisdom and understanding (Colossians 1:9).

When you buy an appliance, you will find a booklet titled "Operating Instructions."

The same is true of the highly sophisticated equipment God designed called men and women. The Bible is God's manual on you. You cannot operate properly until you become acquainted with everything God built into you. The day you invited Jesus into your heart you began a journey that is uniquely yours. Your personality traits and your life experiences have influenced both that moment of decision and your life in Christ since that day.

The Bible details your specifications. God designed you to be filled with the Holy Spirit. If you become filled with a demon spirit or some other foul spirit, you will not function in accordance with God's intentions. That's why a man without God is a dangerous man. He is literally insane. Even though a man's manners may be good, if his spirit is wrong, his behavior will eventually reflect his spirit.

Just as you who were at one time disobedient to God have now received mercy as a result of their disobedience, so they too have now become disobedient in order that they too may now receive mercy as a result of God's mercy to you. For God has bound all men over to disobedience so that He may have mercy on them all (Romans 11:30-32).

Never confuse behavior with regeneration. Your behavior is a result of the conversion of your thinking. Regeneration is the source of that conversion. You cannot demand righteousness from an unrighteous spirit. That's why God gives you His Spirit when you come back to Him. Proper behavior is impossible without the Holy Spirit because your functions arise from the nature of your spirit. If you want to function by love, you have to have the Spirit who is the Source of love.

God has created you with certain features that He has defined and clarified in His Manual. You have a body, a soul, and a spirit. *If you want to operate up to your full potential, you must carefully study how God designed each of these features to function.*

There are certain laws that govern each characteristic. If you disregard these laws, you cannot function properly.

For in Him we live and move and have our being. As some of your own poets have said, "We are His offspring" (Acts 17:28).

Any operating manual for an electronic device describes the *manufacturer's warranty* and the limitations to that warranty. The manufacturer's warranty guarantees that you can return the product to the manufacturer for repair or replacement if the product fails during the specified warranty period. If, however, you violate the warranty limitations, the company is no longer responsible for the equipment. You are. These limitations refer primarily to the operation, environment, and maintenance of the equipment.

God's warranty includes a clause of grace. He'll take you in your wrecked state and throw out satan's parts. Though it may take years, God will continue to work on your memory banks until your mind is cleaned and your life is transformed. Thank God for His grace. He will pay for all the costs to fix you so long as you go to the right dealer. But you can't expect God to fix you if you are going to satan for repair.

The last thing the electronics company tells you in the operating instructions is to *retain the manual for future reference.* In other words, don't throw away your Bibles.

But there is a place where someone has tes-
tified: "What is man that you are mindful of
him, the son of man that you care for him?"
(Hebrews 2:6)

The Bible is the story of God's interaction with humankind. It contains many promises from God to His people, as well as the demands God makes on those who would live in fellowship with Him. God, by sending His Son, shows us the value He places on us. His willingness to send Jesus to die for our sins is the proof of how much we are worth.

When you go to the store to buy a product, you don't put a value on that product. The value of the merchandise was established long before you chose to buy it. When the courtroom of the universe demanded a price for humanity, the value that was placed on the human soul was equal to the death of God. I didn't say the value of the death of God was equal to the human soul. God said, "Whatever it costs to restore the fellowship between men and women and Myself, that's the price I will pay." It's not what is paid that gives value to an item, but what it costs.

*But God demonstrates His own love for us
in this: While we were still sinners, Christ
died for us* (Romans 5:8).

T he boundaries of what God can accomplish
through you were set long before you were born.
He planned your days before you had lived even one
of them (see Ps. 139:16). God wants you to see yourself and your abilities the way He sees you. He puts
great value on you and eagerly encourages each step
you take toward using even a small part of your talents and abilities. God believes in you. The Bible has
much to say about your personal worth and your
unique capabilities.

Throughout the history of mankind, God has
sought to overcome the blindness that sin has
brought to our lives. He watches with sadness as His
creations discount their potential and doubt their
worth. He cries with and for them as they stumble
along, missing the many ways He affirms and con-
firms the valuable persons He created them to be.

God's willingness to send Jesus to die for our
sins is the proof of how much we are worth to Him.

So don't be afraid; you are worth more than many sparrows (Matthew 10:31).

Do you understand how much you are worth? You are equal to the value of your Source. You are as valuable as the God you came from! Stop feeling bad about other people's estimations of your value. You are special. God's word on your potential is the only evaluation that counts. You are not what your teacher or your spouse or your children or your boss say about you. *You are as valuable and capable as God says you are.* If you are going to release your full potential, you must understand and accept the value God places upon you and the confidence He has in your abilities.

Even as God is the One who set your value, so too He is the only One who is qualified to determine the extent of your potential. The possibilities that lie within you are dependent upon God, because the potential of a thing is always determined by the source from which it came. Even as the potential of a wooden table is determined by the strength of the tree from which it was made, so your potential is determined by God, because you came out of God.

But it is the spirit in a man, the breath of the Almighty, that gives him understanding (Job 32:8).

If we examine the stories of man's creation as recorded in Genesis chapters 1 and 2, we discover that God used two kinds of operations when He called the world into being. He *made* things and He *created* things. The Hebrew word for *make* is *asha*, which means "to form out of something that is already there." *Brera*, the Hebrew word for *create*, means "to form out of nothing." It is interesting, then, that Genesis 1:26 says, *"Let Us **make** man in Our image..."* and the following verse says, *"So God **created** man in His own image...."* The creation of man thus involved two different operations.

God *created* man out of nothing, just as He Himself is without a body. Then He formed man's house—our bodies—from the dust of the ground. Man came out of God and is spirit even as God is Spirit. Your body will decay and return to the ground from which it came. Your spirit, which is your true essence, will live forever because spirits cannot die. You share God's eternal Spirit, with all the dreams, aspirations, and desires He contains.

With the tongue we praise our Lord and Father, and with it we curse men, who have been made in God's likeness (James 3:9).

God also created us to operate like He does: *Then God said, "Let Us make man in Our image, in Our likeness..."* (Gen. 1:26).

The Hebrew word translated into the English word *likeness* means "to operate like," not "to look like." God's original design for us requires that we function like God.

God operates by faith. The light in the darkness was not visible before God called it forth, but He believed that light was present in the darkness and, by faith, He spoke it into view. Faith isn't a jump in the dark. It is a walk in the light. Faith is not guessing; it is knowing something.

God made and fashioned you to operate by faith. He designed you to believe the invisible into becoming visible. You may not see what God is calling forth from your life, but God asks you to believe it is there. If you aren't functioning like God, you are malfunctioning. The Manual says, *"The just shall live by faith"* (Rom. 1:17b NKJV), and *"everything that does **not come from faith** is sin* [missing the Manufacturer's standards and expectations]*"* (Rom. 14:23b).

"Everything is permissible for me"—but not everything is beneficial. "Everything is permissible for me"—but I will not be mastered by anything (1 Corinthians 6:12).

G od's perspective on our potential says that we have the power to dominate and subdue the earth.

> *Then God said, "Let Us make man in Our image, in Our likeness, and let them rule over the fish of the sea and the birds of the air, over the livestock, over all the earth, and over all the creatures that move along the ground"* (Genesis 1:26).

Now what does it mean to be a dominator of the earth? It means that the earth should not rule or control us. If you are addicted to cigarettes, you are being controlled by a leaf. If you are ruled by alcohol, you are being controlled by grain. Leaves and grain are the earth. God created you to dominate the earth, not the earth to dominate you. If you are being controlled by any habit, you are submitting to the very things God commands you to dominate.

God has given you the potential to dominate the earth. You have the power to beat whatever habit is ruling you. It's up to you whether you exercise the power God built into you.

By their fruit you will recognize them. Do people pick grapes from thornbushes, or figs from thistles? (Matthew 7:16)

❖

God's perspective on our potential includes dominating, ruling, and subduing the earth. His perspective also sees our potential to multiply. God gave every human being the potential to be fruitful and to reproduce after their kind.

God blessed them and said to them, "Be fruitful and increase in number; fill the earth and subdue it. Rule over the fish of the sea and the birds of the air and over every living creature that moves on the ground (Genesis 1:28).

While it is true that God gave us the ability to have children, the potential God is talking about here is much more than the capacity to have babies. He has given men and women the potential to reproduce what they are. We are producing the next generation.

What kind of children are you producing? God has given you the power to influence them either for good or for evil. Will the next generation be cussing, alcoholic, illiterate people? Or will they be righteous and upright, seeking the Lord, and obeying His commandments? You have the capacity to produce children who mirror your life.

It is God who arms me with strength and makes my way perfect (Psalm 18:32).

The basic principles that apply to the potential of all things also apply to your potential. God, your Source/Creator, is the Definer of your potential. The Bible has much to say about your personal worth and your unique capabilities. You can dominate, rule, and subdue the earth. You can be fruitful and multiply.

God has also given human beings the capacity to imagine and plan and believe anything into reality. That's an awesome potential. The Bible reveals this power in the story of the building of the tower of Babel:

The Lord said, "If as one people speaking the same language they have begun to do this, then nothing they plan to do will be impossible for them" (Genesis 11:6).

In other words, God says, "If I don't interfere, these people will be able to do anything they think about and plan."

God did interfere in the building of that tower, but He didn't stop the people from thinking. He stopped them from understanding one another. You have the potential to think, to imagine, to plan, and to put your plan into action. Anything you carry through from thought to action is within your power to accomplish.

...Everything is possible for him who believes (Mark 9:23).

Consistent with humankind's ability to make plans and bring them to completion is our power to believe impossibilities into possibilities. Jesus said to the father of a demon-possessed boy, *"Everything is possible for him who believes."* This ability is an extension of our potential to operate like God.

The Gospel of Matthew tells a story of faith in which one of Jesus' disciples, for a moment, accomplished the impossible. Peter, with the other disciples, was in a boat on the Sea of Galilee when Jesus came to them, walking on the water. Thinking it was a ghost, the disciples cried out in fear. After Jesus had identified Himself, impetuous Peter replied, *"Lord, if it's You...tell me to come to You on the water"* (Matt. 14:28).

The physical laws of nature should have prevented Peter from walking to Jesus. But the laws of faith are different. When Jesus told him to come, Peter went toward Jesus. Only when he became fearful of the wind and the waves did he begin to sink.

If you are a man or woman of faith, you have the awesome power to operate by the laws of faith. Impossibilities become possibilities when you use this potential.

Then Jesus came to them and said, "All authority in Heaven and on earth has been given to Me" (Matthew 28:18).

Man's tremendous potential includes the capacity to influence both physical and spiritual things. This capacity is a colossal power that we seldom use. Jesus pointed to this power when He told Peter (after Peter had confessed, *"...You are the Christ, the Son of the living God"*), *"I will give you the keys of the kingdom of heaven; whatever you bind on earth will be bound in heaven, and whatever you loose on earth will be loosed in heaven"* (Matt. 16:16,19).

Jesus is encouraging us to look beyond the physical circumstances of our lives to the spiritual dimension. If you are dealing with just the physical aspects of your life, you are missing the real thing. Look beyond the problems in your job or with your spouse or in your church to the spiritual realities that underlie them. Say in the natural what you want to happen in the spiritual. The power to affect both realms is yours. You hold the keys to your effective participation in God's Kingdom, because all authority in Heaven and on earth belongs to Jesus (see Matt. 28:18 above), and He has shared that power with you.

As for you, the anointing you received from Him remains in you, and you do not need anyone to teach you. But as His anointing teaches you about all things and as that anointing is real, not counterfeit—just as it has taught you, remain in Him (1 John 2:27).

W e are continuing to learn how to act like our Source. One principle we need to operate within is in the area of receiving. During His time on earth, Jesus gave His disciples a blank check. He promised them that they could receive whatever they requested.

Therefore I tell you, whatever you ask for in prayer, believe that you have received it, and it will be yours (Mark 11:24).

If you remain in Me and My words remain in you, ask whatever you wish, and it will be given you. This is to My Father's glory, that you bear much fruit, showing your-selves to be My disciples (John 15:7-8).

Jesus cautioned His disciples that the evidence of fruit in their lives would be the indicator that they were His disciples. God is waiting to give you what-ever you request, so long as you sink your roots deep into His Word and allow His words to influence and direct your entire life.

Believe Me when I say that I am in the Father and the Father is in Me; or at least believe on the evidence of the miracles themselves. I tell you the truth, anyone who has faith in Me will do what I have been doing. He will do even greater things than these, because I am going to the Father. And I will do whatever you ask in My name, so that the Son may bring glory to the Father. You may ask Me for anything in My name, and I will do it (John 14:11-14).

During His last days on earth, Jesus spent much time with His disciples teaching them, praying for them, and encouraging them to live in His power. As He spoke of His return to the Father, Jesus assured His disciples that they would continue the work He had begun because they would receive the same power they had witnessed in His ministry (see Acts 1:8).

When Jesus foretold that His disciples would do greater works than He had done, He was talking about the baptism of the Holy Spirit and the power that out-pouring would bring into their lives. What potential!

The grace of our Lord was poured out on me abundantly, along with the faith and love that are in Christ Jesus (1 Timothy 1:14).

———◆◆———

What did it mean when Jesus told His disciples that they would do greater works than He had done? Some people believe that God is afraid we're going to take His job. When we start talking about what we're going to do for God or what we're going to dream, some people say, "You'd better not think bigger than God." Well, you can never be bigger than your Source. *You can't think or plan or imagine something greater than God, because God is the source of your imagination.* He leaked part of His potential into you when He pulled you out of Himself. It's like owning a Sony video cassette recorder with multiple features. It cannot fulfill its purpose or potential until it is plugged into an electrical source. So it is for every person. We must plug into our Source.

Your ability to release your potential is directly related to your knowledge of God and your willingness to stay within the parameters He has established for your relationship with Him.

Be imitators of God, therefore, as dearly loved children (Ephesians 5:1).

Quality is the degree of excellence or the essence of standard that makes one product better than another. The quality of a product can be no better than the qualities of the product's source. You can't use rotten apples to make a delicious apple pie. The pie will reveal the decay in the apples.

The quality of a product can also be defined as the characteristic attributes or elements that determine the product's basic nature. Those qualities arise out of the basic nature of the product's source. Or to say it another way, those things that occur naturally in a product also occur naturally in that from which the product was made.

All the essential qualities that determine who God is and how He acts also determine who you are and how you were designed to act. Your potential is wrapped up in God because His qualities establish yours. When you understand and accept the nature and qualities of God you can begin to understand and accept your nature and qualities.

If you fully obey the Lord your God and carefully follow all His commands I give you today, the Lord your God will set you high above all the nations on earth. All these blessings will come upon you and accompany you if you obey the Lord your God (Deuteronomy 28:1-2).

———————

The death of an old tree is a good word picture to describe the nature of Adam's death. When a large tree is blown down by a hurricane, the tree may lie there for weeks. Although the roots of the tree are torn from the ground and exposed to the air, the tree's leaves do not turn brown as soon as the tree is brought down by the wind. The little sap that was in the roots continues to move up the trunk, out the branches, and into the leaves. When the sap is gone, the leaves turn brown. But the reality of that tree's death occurred when it fell, not when the leaves showed the evidence of its death.

Adam walked around with green leaves but no roots for many years. He was dead long before his body showed the evidence of his death. Unless your life becomes *rerooted in God* through the salvation offered in Jesus Christ, you will die an eternal death. That's the law of God.

So that your faith might not rest on men's wisdom, but on God's power (1 Corinthians 2:5).

Daniel 11:32 promises that *"the people that do know their God shall be strong, and do exploits"* (KJV). This is true because your potential is related to God's potential, and God is *omnipotent*. The combination of *omni* (meaning "always or all full of") and *potent* (meaning "power on reserve"— from which we get the word *potential*) declares that God is always full of power. Or to say it another way, all potential is in God. Thus, people who understand that God contains all the things that He's asking them to do are not afraid to do big things. It's not *what* you know but *who* you know that enables you to do great things with God.

God is God whether you choose to use His potential or not.

When you combine the knowledge of God's omnipotence with the knowledge of who you are in God, you can resist all things that seek to overcome you and wipe out your potential. You can be strong and do great exploits. God is the Source of your potential. He waits to draw from His vast store to enable you to accomplish all that He demands of you.

He replied, "If you have faith as small as a mustard seed, you can say to this mulberry tree, 'Be uprooted and planted in the sea,' and it will obey you" (Luke 17:6).

———————

If I give you a tree as a gift and I tell you it is an avocado tree, you will tell every person who asks you what kind of tree is in your front yard that it's an avocado tree. Now you haven't picked any avocados from that tree, but you still dare to say it's an avocado tree. Why? Because you have faith in me that the tree is what I say it is. You believe that somewhere in that tree there are many avocados. Faith is simply believing and acting on the words and integrity of another. Faith in God is to believe and act on what He says.

What Jesus is really saying is, "Have the God kind of faith." Don't put your faith in your own faith or in the faith of other people or in the mountains or in anything that you expect to happen because of your faith. Put your faith in God, because it's your faith in Him that will accomplish the moving of mountains.

He is the image of the invisible God, the firstborn over all creation. For by Him all things were created: things in Heaven and on earth, visible and invisible, whether thrones or powers or rulers or authorities; all things were created by Him and for Him (Colossians 1:15-16).

Hebrews 1:3 tells us, *"The Son is the radiance of God's glory and the exact representation of His being, sustaining all things by His powerful Word...."* The King James Version of this verse says that Jesus upholds all things *"by the Word of His power...."* Not the *power of His Word*, but the *Word of His power*. God's power is released in you when you stay alive with His Word.

By taking us out of Himself, God decreed that our lives must be maintained by Him. As long as we obey God's requirement, His power is released within us and we know abundant life. That is why the writer to the Hebrews describes Jesus as the "Word of God's power." There's power in God's Word if we keep it. Jesus, through His obedience unto death, released for us the power of God's Word that brings eternal life.

*He cuts off every branch in Me that bears
no fruit, while every branch that does bear
fruit He prunes so that it will be even more
fruitful* (John 15:2).
*...No branch can bear fruit by itself; it must
remain in the vine. Neither can you bear
fruit unless you remain in Me* (John 15:4).

*I*f you cut yourself off from God, your potential is
aborted. No matter how hard you try to plant
yourself in other organizations and activities, God
says, "You are dead." Even if you plant yourself in
religion, you are dead unless you know God and
draw your nutrients from Him.

*Our need for God is not an alternative or an
option.* Like the plants and the animals, which cannot be maintained without the soil, and the fish,
which cannot live outside the water, *we cannot flourish and bear fruit apart from God.* When Jesus says
in John 14:6, *"I am the way, the truth and the life,"*
He isn't trying to convince us that He's the *best* way.
He didn't use that word. Life rooted in God is a
necessity. There is no option.

And I will ask the Father, and He will give you another Counselor to be with you forever (John 14:16).

When Jesus told His disciples that He was going away, He promised them that the Holy Spirit would come to be with them forever. Moments before His ascension to Heaven, Jesus also promised that the *power of the Holy Spirit* (see Acts 1:8) would equip His followers to be His messengers.

Is the Holy Spirit present in your life? Are you flowing in a consistent, empowering relationship that undergirds your every thought, dream, and plan? Or are you trying to do great things without the power of the Spirit?

We may see a skyscraper or a space shuttle or a fancy computer and say, "That's something else. Man is really working here." But the Spirit says, "That's nothing compared to what people could do. That's what people are doing without Me. I want you to do something people cannot do unless they have Me. I want you to build people. I have the stuff to empower you to help people build new foundations and open new windows through which to see life. I want to give you a view from the top of life so you can see the way God sees."

You, dear children, are from God and have overcome them, because the One who is in you is greater than the one who is in the world (1 John 4:4).

———◆———

In Philippians 4:13 Paul says, "I can do everything through Him who gives me strength."

You cannot do *all things*. You can only do *all things* through *Christ*, who gives you the ability. Even though you may shout to everybody, "I can do all things," God is asking you, "Are you with Christ?" Because if you're not, your plans, dreams, and imaginations will amount to nothing. Without Christ your efforts are futile and the result is frustration.

If you are going to release your potential, you must live each day checking out who's *with* you instead of who's against you. You can spend the rest of your life fighting the many people and circumstances that come against you, or you can focus on God's presence and treat them as a temporary inconvenience. If God is with you, those who accuse or harass you have no power over you.

...In this world you will have trouble. But take heart! I have overcome the world (John 16:33).

For the wages of sin is death, but the gift of God is eternal life in Christ Jesus our Lord (Romans 6:23).

Humans have become experts at understanding how plants and animals function. We cross-breed animals to create strains that are stronger, tastier, and more productive. We graft stock from one tree to another to develop more compact trees that yield tastier fruit that grow larger and keep longer. But we are deficient in our understanding and application of how God designed humans to function. We concentrate on our bodies instead of our spirits. This situation seriously threatens our ability to release our potential.

Man in his fallen state could no longer know and understand the thoughts and purposes of God. He became controlled by his soul instead of his spirit and began to look to his environment for the information he needed.

All human beings since Adam sin: *"For all have sinned and fall short of the glory of God..."* (Rom. 3:23). We bear in our spirits, souls, and bodies the penalty of his disobedience. You were born spiritually dead or paralyzed, and your body will eventually die. Your brain, apart from God, can know no more than those who teach you or those who write the books you read.

"Are you still so dull?" Jesus asked them. "Don't you see that whatever enters the mouth goes into the stomach and then out of the body? But the things that come out of the mouth come from the heart, and these make a man 'unclean.' For out of the heart come evil thoughts, murder, adultery, sexual immorality, theft, false testimony, slander. These are what make a man 'unclean'" (Matthew 15:16-20a).

The desire to steal or covet is prompted by what you see with your physical eyes, and your sexual desires are provoked by the physical wants of your body. Indeed, life from the body discourages respect and encourages behavior that regards men and women as objects to be conquered. We treat people like products to be manipulated instead of images of Christ to be cherished and honored.

God has a name for those who detach themselves from Him and live from the body. He calls them "mere dirt." Now that's an insult. Anyone who doesn't know God is a mere person. A mere person does things unnaturally. Because they don't know their Creator and the purposes and desires He had when He created them, they focus on their *made* beings—that which came from the dust—instead of their *created* beings—that which came from God.

Therefore, there is now no condemnation for those who are in Christ Jesus, because through Christ Jesus the law of the Spirit of life set me free from the law of sin and death (Romans 8:1-2).

You were originally God's property, but satan stole you from God. Jesus paid the redemptive price through death on the cross so you could be restored to eternal life and fellowship with God. When Jesus saved you from sin and death, He rekindled your potential by giving you His Holy Spirit to live in you and to be connected to your spirit.

God's in the business of giving you a new body. So don't worry if this body isn't all you'd like it to be. Patch it, fix it, do whatever you can to spruce it up. *But don't equate your life with your body.* God's going to get out of you all that He put in you. He wants you to start releasing your potential with the body you now have and to continue using your eternal capabilities long after this body has decayed. *You are much more than your imperfect, deteriorating body.*

God's going to get out of you all that He put in you.

...Forgetting what is behind and straining toward what is ahead, I press on toward the goal to win the prize for which God has called me heavenward in Christ Jesus (Philippians 3:13-14).

G od thinks in terms of potential—of things that are not yet manifested. He relies on what He knows isn't visible yet, instead of what is visible. He is not excited by what you've already done.

God's waiting for your potential to be revealed. He says, "You are not what you are acting like. Because you are My child, you have the potential to act better than you're acting. My potential is flowing from Me to you."

Many of us don't appreciate how faith works. We are so used to living from what we can see, hear, and touch that we have great difficulty moving into the realm of faith. If, for example, someone asks us how we are doing, we usually respond based on the condition of our bodies or our souls. We focus on our illnesses or the depressed thoughts that are weighing us down and neglect to mention the many blessings God has promised us. These promises have a much greater impact on our lives than our physical diseases and our emotional struggles.

It is written: "I believed; therefore I have spoken." With that same spirit of faith we also believe and therefore speak, because we know that the one who raised the Lord Jesus from the dead will also raise us with Jesus and present us with you in His presence (2 Corinthians 4:13-14).

Faith begins with *belief.* Actually, faith in someone or something requires unquestioning belief that does not require proof or evidence from the one in whom you have faith.

Faith requires putting your body under the control of your spirit. Your body says, "I'm not going to believe it until I see it." But God says, "If you're going to operate like Me, you aren't going to see it until you believe it!" One operates by sight, the other by faith.

Living by faith also requires that you put your soul under the control of your spirit. Your soul governs your emotions, your will, and your mind. When you live from your soul, you allow information from your physical body to govern your decisions.

Faith is required of all who want to please God.

Jesus replied, "I tell you the truth, if you have faith and do not doubt, not only can you do what was done to the fig tree, but also you can say to this mountain, 'Go, throw yourself into the sea,' and it will be done" (Matthew 21:21).

Faith is not an option for the Christian. It is a necessity. If God tells you to get moving, He doesn't want you to stand around until you see the evidence that says you should get moving. He wants you to risk, simply because He is asking you to move.

In fact, faith is not an option for human beings in general. A person who lives on anything but faith is going to live a depressing life. Faith is the source of hope, and no man can live without hope. Faith is the fuel of the future and the energy of anticipation.

Faith is the catalyst that makes things happen. It lifts you above the outward evidence of your life and empowers you to bring light out of darkness. Remember, you will receive whatever you believe. If you expect trouble, you will get it. If you trust God and expect Him to work in the midst of your distressing circumstances, sooner or later you will see evidence of His presence.

I have been crucified with Christ and I no longer live, but Christ lives in me. The life I live in the body, I live by faith in the Son of God, who loved me and gave Himself for me (Galatians 2:20).

If things aren't working out for you, there's probably something wrong with your believing, conceiving, or speaking. Stop being intimidated by evil influences or the wicked one. Because he doesn't want you to live by faith, the evil one tries to convince you to believe wrong, conceive wrong, and speak wrong so there's no way you can receive what you have believed. Refuse to believe his lies and be careful not to worry about the criticisms and objections of others. *If God is the source of your dream, people cannot destroy it.* You *can* accomplish what God wills.

Look for the positive in life and renew your voice of faith. Trust in the certainty that you can't lose when you and God are in agreement, and bear in mind that God will reward you if you put Him above all else. Commit yourself to believing, conceiving, and releasing (speaking) every day until you receive what you desire. That's how God created you to function.

In Him we were also chosen, having been predestined according to the plan of Him who works out everything in conformity with the purpose of His will (Ephesians 1:11).

———◆———

Saul was a zealous Jew who intensely persecuted the early Church and tried to destroy it. But God had another plan for Saul's life, of which Saul was ignorant. God had set Saul apart before his birth *"to reveal His Son in* [him] *so that* [he] *might preach Him among the Gentiles"* (Gal. 1:16). On the road to Damascus, Saul came face to face with the purpose for which God had created him. That encounter changed Saul's life forever. Saul the Pharisee became Paul the apostle.

Although the encounter with your purpose need not be as dramatic as Saul's was, you too need to discover the purpose for which God created you. I've met many successful people who have been dissatisfied with their accomplishments. They have pursued goals and met them, but they have no fulfillment and continually ask why. Accomplishments without a sense of purpose are meaningless. Life without an understanding of life's purpose leads to disillusionment and emptiness.

So I tell you this, and insist on it in the Lord, that you must no longer live as the Gentiles do, in the futility of their thinking (Ephesians 4:17).

———◆———

J esus had an attitude toward purpose. That attitude is expressed in the words of the apostle Paul in First Corinthians 2:11:

For who among men knows the thoughts of a man except the man's spirit within him? In the same way, no one knows the thoughts of God except the Spirit of God.

Since you were born separated from God and out of touch with His Spirit, you are ignorant. Jesus pointed to the spiritual ignorance of man when He preached repentance (see Matt. 4:17). Jesus knew that admission into the Kingdom of Heaven required this complete change in thinking. His command to repent initiated God's new work of grace. Many of the religious leaders were offended by Jesus' preaching.

The truth is, no matter how you are thinking before you meet Jesus, your thinking is wrong. Without God you are ignorant: *"They are darkened in their understanding and separated from the life of God because of the ignorance that is in them due to the hardening of their hearts"* (Eph. 4:18).

[God] *will punish those who do not know God and do not obey the gospel of our Lord Jesus. They will be punished with everlasting destruction and shut out from the presence of the Lord and from the majesty of His power* (2 Thessalonians 1:8-9).

Without Jesus you cannot come to God: *"I am the way and the truth and the life. No one comes to the Father except through Me"* (John 14:6). Life apart from God leads to destruction.

God doesn't want you to *perish*. Out of His great love and mercy, God provides repentance as the means by which you can avoid destruction. If you don't want to be destroyed by ignorance of God and His purpose for your life, you have to change your way of thinking.

Ignorance robs you of your potential because it leads to abuse. You can't use something in its natural way unless you know why it exists and how it was designed to be used.

If a man doesn't know the purpose of a wife, he'll abuse her. If a woman doesn't know what a husband is for, she'll abnormally use him. And of course, the greatest tragedy occurs when people don't know what children are for and they abuse them.

Many are the plans in a man's heart, but it is the Lord's purpose that prevails (Proverbs 19:21).

We must go back to the mind of our Manufacturer to find out the purpose for our existence. Nobody knows the product like the creator, no matter who the creator is. If you built a house, you know where you used old wood that nobody else can see because it's covered by paint.

You are related to where you came from. That means nobody knows you like the One from whom you came. God who created you knows how He designed you to operate. He wants you to understand His thoughts toward you and His purposes for your life. If you try to live without God, you will completely mess up your life, because life without purpose brings abuse.

Look around you. Many people have food, houses, cars, friends, mothers, fathers, and families that they are abusing. They don't know the purpose of these people and things so they keep abusing them. If you don't know the purpose of a product, ask its manufacturer. If you don't know the purpose of your family and friends, go to God. Knowledge of purpose is the only way to avoid abuse.

If I give all I possess to the poor and surrender my body to the flames, but have not love, I gain nothing (1 Corinthians 13:3).

First Corinthians chapter 13 is an example of how we can abuse things if we don't know their purpose. People just love this chapter, but they have a hard time living it. Why? Because they fail to look at the verses that precede it, which talk about the baptism of the Holy Spirit.

There are different kinds of gifts, but the same Spirit....Now to each one the manifestation of the Spirit is given for the common good....All these are the work of one and the same Spirit, and He gives them to each one, just as He determines....And now I will show you the most excellent way.... Love is patient, love is kind... (1 Corinthians 12:4,7,11,31b; 13:4a).

If we don't have the Holy Spirit in our lives, we will abuse love and those we desire to love. Without Him we will be impatient, unkind, envious, boastful, proud, rude, self-seeking, and easily angered in our relationships with our loved ones. In fact, our love will fail because we don't understand love as an outgrowth of God's power in our lives. When we receive the manifestation of the Holy Spirit, God's love can operate through us.

The people living in darkness have seen a great light; on those living in the land of the shadow of death a light has dawned (Matthew 4:16).

━━━◆━━━

Psalm 82 describes man's situation without God:

They know nothing, they understand nothing. They walk about in darkness; all the foundations of the earth are shaken. I said, "You are 'gods'; you are all sons of the Most High." But you will die like mere men... (Psalm 82:5-7a).

Confusion and abuse characterize the lives of those who do not understand why God created them. They are completely without purpose and direction. They don't know anything. They don't understand anything. They (and their world) are totally out of line going nowhere fast. This can be our lot as well. Even if we are children of the Most High, we may be living like mere flesh and blood who have not received the Spirit of God.

You may think God created you to get a good education or to go to church or to make a living. In truth, none of those achieve God's purpose for creating you. God created you:

- To express His image.
- To enjoy fellowship with Him.
- To dominate the earth.
- To bear fruit.
- To reproduce yourself.

For those God foreknew He also predestined to be conformed to the likeness of His Son, that He might be the firstborn among many brothers (Romans 8:29).

If you don't know your purpose, it is impossible to fulfill it. Thus the release of your potential requires that you learn why God created you. The Bible clearly defines God's reasons for creating human beings:

- *To express God's image.*
- To enjoy fellowship with God.
- To dominate the earth.
- To bear fruit.
- To reproduce ourselves.

Everything you are is related to your purpose—your height, race, natural talents, gifts, and deep desires. God created you to express His image. He did not create you so you could hate yourself so much that you try to change what you look like. Fashionable clothes, cosmetics, and hairstyles are fine so long as you know why you are choosing to look like you do. If you just want to look your best, then go for it. But if you are trying to look like someone else, you're in big trouble. God doesn't want you to look like someone else. He wants you to look like you and act like Him.

Through these He has given us His very great and precious promises, so that through them you may participate in the divine nature and escape the corruption in the world caused by evil desires (2 Peter 1:4).

Let's continue to look at God's reasons for creating human beings:

- *To express God's image.*
- To enjoy fellowship with God.
- To dominate the earth.
- To bear fruit.
- To reproduce ourselves.

Expressing God's image has to do with the way you act, not the way you look. He wants you to mirror His character. He fashioned you so that His nature could be revealed through your uniqueness.

The essence of God's nature is succinctly defined in the "love" chapter we looked at earlier. Here are the wonderful things this chapter describes.

[God] *is patient,* [God] *is kind.* [He] *does not envy,* [He] *does not boast,* [He] *is not proud.* [God] *is not rude,* [He] *is not self-seeking,* [He] *is not easily angered,* [He] *keeps no record of wrongs.* [God] *does not delight in evil but rejoices with the truth.* [God] *always protects, always trusts, always hopes, always perseveres.* [God] *never fails* (1 Corinthians 13:4-8a).

God is spirit, and His worshipers must worship in spirit and in truth (John 4:24).

Here are God's reasons for creating human beings:

- To express God's image.
- *To enjoy fellowship with God.*
- To dominate the earth.
- To bear fruit.
- To reproduce ourselves.

God's first question to Adam after Adam's disobedience was *"Where are you?"* (see Gen. 3:9). God had come to the Garden in the cool of the day to enjoy fellowship with the man and the woman He had created. The opportunity for fellowship was part of the reason God had created human beings.

Fellowship is companionship—a mutual sharing of an experience, an activity, or an interest. You cannot enjoy fellowship with God unless you have received Jesus as your Savior, because sinful human beings cannot know and understand God's experiences, activities, and interests. A reconnection of God's Spirit and your spirit is the prerequisite for the establishment of this companionship. The fulfillment of your purpose to love God and enjoy Him forever is impossible until you reclaim your spiritual heritage, for those who seek to worship God must worship Him in spirit and in truth (see John 4:24).

You have made him to have dominion over the works of Your hands; You have put all things under his feet (Psalm 8:6 NKJV).

<hr>

We are continuing to study God's reasons for creating human beings:

- To express God's image.
- To enjoy fellowship with God.
- *To dominate the earth.*
- To bear fruit.
- To reproduce ourselves.

Then God said, "Let Us make man in Our image, in Our likeness, and let them rule over the fish of the sea and the birds of the air, over the livestock, over all the earth, and over all the creatures that move along the ground" (Genesis 1:26).

God created us to dominate the entire earth. But when we lost touch with our Source, we became confused and allowed the earth to dominate us. Every problem that we are experiencing is the result of our not fulfilling our purpose to dominate the earth. But more serious than the domination itself is the deception that goes along with the domination. We are tremendous self-deceivers. Reconnect with your Source and allow God to show you who you really are.

The wrath of God is being revealed from heaven against all the godlessness and wickedness of men who suppress the truth by their wickedness (Romans 1:18).

The lack of knowledge or the loss of insight into the purpose of a person or a thing always leads to confusion and pain. Homosexuality is an excellent example of the resulting turmoil. God created the woman to be a suitable helpmeet to the man. Anything else is abnormal use.

The apostle Paul spoke of this abnormality when he wrote to the church at Rome:

The wrath of God is being revealed from Heaven against all the godlessness and wickedness of men who suppress the truth by their wickedness...For although they knew God, they neither glorified Him as God nor gave thanks to Him, but their thinking became futile and their foolish hearts were darkened....Because of this, God gave them over to shameful lusts. Even their women exchanged natural relations for unnatural ones. In the same way the men also abandoned natural relations with women and were inflamed with lust for one another... (Romans 1:18,21,26-27).

God abhors abnormal use. He destroyed the cities of Sodom and Gomorrah for such evil (see Gen. 18-19). Satan, on the other hand, wants us to justify our sin by thinking it is natural.

Christ came to set us free from sin and bring us back to His original purpose for us.

This to My Father's glory, that you bear much fruit, showing yourselves to be My disciples....You did not choose Me, but I chose you and appointed you to go and bear fruit—fruit that will last (John 15:8,16a).

Review God's reasons for creating human beings:

- To express God's image.
- To enjoy fellowship with God.
- To dominate the earth.
- *To bear fruit.*
- To reproduce ourselves.

Jesus teaches us in the Gospel of John that God created us to bear fruit (see above). Your fruitfulness is related to the food you are eating. If your spiritual source is not of top quality, your productivity will show it. No matter where you go or what you do, apart from God you will be an ornamental plant without fruit. You are what you eat.

But the fruit of the Spirit is love, joy, peace, patience, kindness, goodness, faithfulness, gentleness and self-control. Against such things there is no law. Those who belong to Christ Jesus have crucified the sinful nature with its passions and desires. Since we live by the Spirit, let us keep in step with the Spirit (Galatians 5:22-25).

You can feed on the fruit of the Spirit.

Anyone who believes in the Son of God has this testimony in his heart. Anyone who does not believe God has made him out to be a liar, because he has not believed the testimony God has given about His Son (1 John 5:10).

We continue to study God's reasons for creating human beings:

- To express God's image.
- To enjoy fellowship with God.
- To dominate the earth.
- To bear fruit.
- *To reproduce ourselves.*

God created you to multiply and replenish the earth (see Gen. 1:28). This ability to have children is sometimes seen as a curse rather than a blessing. Sin is at the root of these feelings.

...I will greatly increase your pains in childbearing; with pain you will give birth to children. Your desire will be for your husband, and he will rule over you (Genesis 3:16).

But more important than your ability to physically reproduce is your power to instill in others your values and attitudes. Your life influences your children, your spouse, your friends, your boss, your coworkers, and so on, for good or evil. They watch your actions and hear your words. The effect of your presence in their lives can be either discouraging or encouraging, degrading or upbuilding, negative or positive.

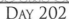

Who, by the power that enables Him to bring everything under His control, will transform our lowly bodies so that they will be like His glorious body (Philippians 3:21).

The release of your potential is directly related to your willingness to know, understand, and submit to God's purposes for your life. The wisdom and power to accomplish this task is available to all who have the gift of God's indwelling Spirit. For He is the channel through which you can freely communicate with God until your heart and vision become one with His.

The corollary is also true. Life apart from God subjects you to control by other things, people, and spirits and conceals the purpose for which you were born. Under those circumstances, you and your potential will be abused. Indeed, much that you have to offer will die with you.

Take time now to examine your life. Who or what is controlling you? Are you releasing your potential by discovering God's purpose for your life?

You have the ability to fulfill that purpose because God built it into you. Determine now to find God's intent for your life.

Do not love sleep or you will grow poor;
stay awake and you will have food to spare
(Proverbs 20:13).

Most of us at some point in our lives have wished that we had more resources than we actually have. We have looked at another person's resources and envied them, bemoaning our apparent poverty. This attitude is a stumbling block to releasing our full potential because God's view of poverty and wealth is very different from ours.

The poor man and the oppressor have this
in common: The Lord gives sight to the eyes
of both (Proverbs 29:13).

Therefore, it is not that God makes rich people and poor people. Rather God makes all people—some who become rich and some who become poor. The key is what you do with the resources God gives you.

Lazy hands make a man poor, but diligent
hands bring wealth (Proverbs 10:4).

Poverty is a not a gift from God but the result of your actions. The degree of wealth or poverty in which you find yourself is to a large extent related to the way you are using what you have.

And my God will meet all your needs according to His glorious riches in Christ Jesus (Philippians 4:19).

God created a potent man (Adam) and supplied him with resources with unlimited potential. Nothing we have today was added to or subtracted from God's original provisions in the Garden. But those resources are not equally divided among the peoples of our world. Hardworking, diligent people got their hands on most of the wealth, while lazy, sluggardly people watched them take it. Thus, our world knows the rich, the poor, and those who are in transit—some gaining wealth and others losing it.

If you learn what your resources are and how they were designed to operate, you will have limitless potential. But if you use them in an abnormal way, you will destroy your potential.

Cocaine, for example, is used in hospitals to bring healing. But if people misuse it, their thinking will be distorted and they'll end up losing many of the things that are dear to them. Or consider drugs like aspirin and Tylenol, which relieve pain. If these drugs are used according to the directions on the bottle, they have a positive influence. But if the warning to limit their use is disregarded, they can kill or make people very ill.

God is life-giving…His mercy and peace has no end.

In order that satan might not outwit us. For we are not unaware of his schemes (2 Corinthians 2:11).

O ne of the greatest problems facing the Church is not the lack of resources but the *lack of use* of resources. Every resource God gave to Adam is available to us. But we don't use all those resources. Instead of seeing the possibilities in everything God has given us, we categorize our resources and refuse to use some of them because we are threatened by the world's use of them.

What the world is doing or building is not the problem. Worldly people don't have any more resources than those they are currently using to solve the world's problems. This is not true for the Church. The Church is not solving the world's problems because we misunderstand the resources that are available to us.

The Scriptures are clear that God is the Creator and satan is a perverter. Satan cannot create anything. He can only pervert what God created. Therein lies the source of our problem. Counterfeits abound in our world. They are the result of satan's misuse and abuse of God's resources.

In the next few days we'll be looking at the types of resources God has given us to use.

...Man does not live on bread alone, but on every word that comes from the mouth of God (Matthew 4:4).

<hr>

There are five types of resources you must understand and control if you are going to become a successful person:

1. Spiritual.
2. Physical.
3. Material.
4. The soul.
5. Time.

Spiritual Resources

First, God has given you spiritual resources. Because God created you in His own image, He gave you the ability to tap into Him. Spiritual food is available to you in a variety of forms. First and foremost, you must feed your spirit from the Word of God.

Find a good place where they teach the Word of God. Keep staying there until you get what they are feeding you. You may fall as you learn to walk according to the Spirit, but that's OK. Just pick yourself up and try again. As long as you're feeding yourself spiritual food, you're growing, changing, and getting stronger. You may not see that growth, but it's happening whether you see it or not.

Then God said, "I give you every seed-bearing plant on the face of the whole earth and every tree that has fruit with seed in it. They will be yours for food" (Genesis 1:29).

We will continue to study the five types of resources you must understand and control if you are going to become a successful person: spiritual, physical, material, the soul, and time.

Physical Resources

God's provisions include physical resources. When God created you, He created your spirit and put it into your body. Because of God's gift of life, your wonderful, physical machine can breathe, move, eat, and heal itself. You can see the beauty of flowers, a sunset, or a rainbow. You can taste the sweetness of honey or of fruit fresh from the tree. Choose carefully the kind of fuel you give your body. Be aware that your body is for food, and food is for your body. Like any of God's resources, improper care and inappropriate attitudes toward your body can result in misuse and abuse (see 1 Cor. 6:12-13,15a).

Material Resources

The third kind of resource God has given you is material resources. God's conversation with Adam in the Garden of Eden shows that God provided well for Adam's needs (see Gen. 1:29 above).

What good will it be for a man if he gains the whole world, yet forfeits his soul? Or what can a man give in exchange for his soul? (Matthew 16:26)

W̱e are studying the five types of resources you must understand and control if you are going to become a successful person: spiritual, physical, material, the soul, and time.

The Resources of the Soul

You are spirit and you have a soul. The assistance you receive from your mind, your will, and your feelings are the resources of the soul that God has given you. The Scriptures recognize the importance of the soul: *"Dear friends, I urge you, as aliens and strangers in the world, to abstain from sinful desires, which war against your soul"* (1 Pet. 2:11). The resources of your soul become available to you when you allow God to transform your mind.

The Resource of the Time

Time is a temporary interruption in eternity. It is a commodity that can be neither bought nor sold. The only thing you can do with time is use it. If you don't use it, you lose it.

Say, "God, I am going to use every minute of my day constructively, effectively, and efficiently."

For surely, O Lord, you bless the righteous;
You surround them with Your favor as with
a shield (Psalm 5:12).

God provides many resources beyond those of spirit, body, material things, soul, and time to challenge your potential. How are you using these resources? Or are you even aware that you have these assets?

God wants to enlarge your vision of what you have. He wants you to see the storehouses of blessing that presently surround you. Use the anointing God has poured upon the Church and its ministers. Move beyond your shame and let them minister to your needs. Spend time reading God's Word until the Bible becomes for you a treasure of knowledge and inspiration.

No matter how rich or poor you are financially, you are accountable to God for the wealth of your resources. You have the responsibility to discover, enhance, and cultivate the precious gifts you have received from God's hand. He carefully scrutinizes your attitudes and anxiously watches your use (or abuse) of the resources He has given you.

For everyone who has will be given more,
and he will have an abundance. Whoever
does not have, even what he has will be
taken from him (Matthew 25:29).

*He also says, "In the beginning, O Lord,
You laid the foundations of the earth, and
the heavens are the work of your hands"*
(Hebrews 1:10).

Y ou are what you eat, and what's eating you.

The story is told of a small boy who wanted to play with his pet fish. So he reached into the fish tank, caught the squirming fish, and placed it on the floor beside him. Then he returned to playing with the cars and trucks that were scattered on the floor around him. Many minutes later, he remembered the fish and turned toward his pet. The fish no longer moved when he touched it.

When his mother saw the fish, she quickly took it and put it in the fish tank. The boy watched tearfully as his pet floated on the top of the water. It was dead. Compassionately, the mother replied, "Honey, didn't you know that the fish can't live on the floor? God made fish to live in water."

This story illustrates how much God's creatures depend on the correct environment to live and grow.

"Whether He is a sinner or not, I don't know. One thing I do know. I was blind but now I see! ...Nobody has ever heard of opening the eyes of a man born blind. If this man were not from God, He could do nothing" (John 9:25,32-33).

———— ◆ ————

Violation of environment always produces death. Vegetation that is planted in parched ground will eventually wither and decay. Wildlife that lives in areas of drought will die from dehydration and starvation. Fish that live in polluted waters will become sickly and die. The Bible tells a story that illustrates this principle.

Jesus was called to the home of a ruler whose daughter had died. When He entered the house, Jesus found that the professional mourners had arrived and the funeral, with its cacophony of sounds, was in progress. After He had put the noisy crowd outside, Jesus entered the room where the girl lay. In the quietness, He took her by the hand and she got up. The unbelief and mockery of the crowd produced the wrong environment for a resurrection, so Jesus changed the environment.

Now the Lord God had planted a garden in the east, in Eden; and there He put the man He had formed. And the Lord God made all kinds of trees grow out of the ground—trees that were pleasing to the eye and good for food. In the middle of the garden were the tree of life and the tree of the knowledge of good and evil. A river watering the garden flowed from Eden (Genesis 2:8-10a).

Everything was designed to function within a specific environment. The conditions of that environment are the specifications that affect the creature's ability to fulfill its purpose. If your environment is ideal, the possibilities for fulfilling your potential are limitless.

God planted a treasure in you. That treasure will be released when you learn the conditions of your ideal environment and make the effort to keep your environment in line with those conditions. God set your ideal environment when He created a garden in Eden and put Adam in the Garden.

An examination of the Garden's description reveals that:

1. God created the Garden.
2. God planted the Garden.
3. God organized the Garden.
4. God's presence was in the Garden.
5. God provided everything man needed to live in the Garden, including faith.

The eye is the lamp of the body. If your eyes are good, your whole body will be full of light. But if your eyes are bad, your whole body will be full of darkness (Matthew 6:22-23a).

Our present world is designed to destroy your potential. This attack on your environment has been around since Adam and Eve experienced similar pressures in the Garden.

Satan's attack came as mental pollution: "Did God really say…?" When the woman repeated what God had said, the serpent went one step further to devastate the woman's faith in God and His words:

"You will not surely die," the serpent said to the woman. "For God knows that when you eat of it your eyes will be opened, and you will be like God, knowing good and evil" (Genesis 3:4-5).

Thus, the serpent completely undermined the woman's faith in God. The progression of the corruption that controlled Eve also seeks to ensnare you. Pollution starts with the eyes. Seeing isn't sinning, and looking won't kill you. Seeing is the opening through which sinful thoughts and actions begin to take hold. If you don't want to eat, don't look.

God doesn't have to convict you of sin because the polluted atmosphere of guilt and excuses will.

Take a few moments now to allow the Holy Spirit to convict you of any area where you may have allowed pollution into your life. He will deliver you.

The wrath of God is being revealed from heaven against all the godlessness and wickedness of men who suppress the truth by their wickedness, since what may be known about God is plain to them, because God has made it plain to them. For since the creation of the world God's invisible qualities—His eternal power and divine nature—have been clearly seen, being understood from what has been made, so that men are without excuse (Romans 1:18-20).

After their banishment from the Garden, Adam and Eve entered a world gone awry. The first evidence of this confusion emerges when Cain murders his brother, Abel. Several generations later, we again see the dysfunction that arises from a polluted environment. Lamech, one of Cain's descendants, marries two women (see Gen. 4:19) and unfaithfulness enters the world.

By the time of Noah, the world was so out of control that *"The Lord saw how great man's wickedness on the earth had become, and that every inclination of the thoughts of his heart was only evil all the time"* (Gen. 6:5). So grieved was God by this situation that He destroyed the earth and nearly all people.

Do not love the world or anything in the world. If anyone loves the world, the love of the Father is not in him....The world and its desires pass away, but the man who does the will of God lives forever (1 John 2:15,17).

Jesus told a story that points to the solution of our messed up environment: A father had two sons. One day not long after he had asked his father for his share of the inheritance, the younger son left home and went to a distant country where he wasted his wealth in wild living. After he had spent everything, he became so hungry that he longed to eat the pigs' food.

When he came to his senses, he said, "How many of my father's hired men have food to spare, and here I am starving to death!"... So he got up and went to his father (Luke 15:17-20a).

What a telling phrase: *"When he came to his senses..."* It reveals both the son's awareness of his poverty and his belief that his need could be met. He trusted his father's goodness enough to return and ask for forgiveness.

God is well acquainted with the insanity of your world. He offers Himself as the solution to your problems—Jesus.

These commandments that I give you today are to be upon your hearts. Impress them on your children. Talk about them when you sit at home and when you walk along the road...Write them on the doorframes of your houses and on your gates (Deuteronomy 6:6-7,9).

Take a few moments to examine your environment. Is it uplifting or degrading? Does it enrich your spiritual life or detract from the work of God's Spirit in your heart? Is obedience to God the norm for those with whom you spend your days or do rebellion and disobedience characterize the lifestyles of your closest friends?

A Checklist for Your Environmental Conditions:
1. Who are your friends?
2. What books do you read?
3. What movies do you watch?
4. What magazines fill your shelves?
5. What are your hobbies?
6. What are your recreational activities?
7. Who feeds your musical appetites?
8. Who are your heroes?
9. Who feeds you spiritually?
10. Are the conditions of your home, school, work, or play conducive to your goals in life?

All the above should be carefully screened, analyzed, and adjusted to feed, activate, enhance, and foster the release of your potential.

Misfortune pursues the sinner, but prosperity is the reward of the righteous. A good man leaves an inheritance for his children's children, but a sinner's wealth is stored up for the righteous (Proverbs 13:21-22).

Many workers see their jobs as dull, laborious, repetitious, tedious, and irritating. This attitude toward work has become of great concern to governments, corporations, and the media. As major problems with poor quality work, reduced productivity, and declining services cripple economic growth, the need and the desire to offer incentives and motivational exercises grow. Thus, benefits such as aerobics classes, fitness rooms, and running tracks have become the focus of much effort and expense in the work place.

No matter how we dissect things, the power in our society can be reduced to two basic elements: *God* and *money*. We are either working for one or the other.

No one can serve two masters. Either he will hate the one and love the other, or he will be devoted to the one and despise the other. You cannot serve both God and Money (Matthew 6:24).

Which one you serve has a significant impact on the release of your potential, because the basic power in your life determines what motivates you. If money motivates you, greed will control your actions. If God empowers you, His purposes for your life will control you.

The wages of the righteous bring them life, but the income of the wicked brings them punishment (Proverbs 10:16).

The love of money promotes corrupt morals and perverted values. The need to accumulate more and more material wealth overshadows God's concerns of truth and honesty until deception and dishonesty determine what we do and how we do it.

The wicked man earns deceptive wages, but he who sows righteousness reaps a sure reward....Whoever trusts in his riches will fall, but the righteous will thrive like a green leaf (Proverbs 11:18,28).

This conflict between God and money is very evident in our attitudes toward work.

Most of us want jobs, but we don't want to work. We want the money, but we don't want to expend the energy. Nothing is as depressing and frustrating as having someone on a job who's not interested in working.

This attitude is completely contrary to God's concept of work. God wants you to be a good worker, not a good job keeper. He is more interested in your attitude toward work than the status of your checkbook. He has the power to increase your bank account balance, but it is up to you to have a positive attitude toward work.

Moreover, when God gives any man wealth and possessions, and enables him to enjoy them, to accept his lot and be happy in his work—this is a gift of God (Ecclesiastes 5:19).

Thomas Edison was a great inventor. Many of the things we enjoy today, including the electric light, are the fruit of his willingness to be responsible for the possibilities hidden within him. His life mirrored his words: "Genius is 1 percent inspiration, 99 percent perspiration."

Too often we allow the pain and perspiration of work to hide its blessings. We assume that work is a necessary evil without looking for the good it brings. The source of our misconceptions lies in the fact that we equate sin and work. Although work does not exist because of sin, sin did change the conditions of work.

Cursed is the ground because of you; through painful toil you will eat of it all the days of your life. It will produce thorns and thistles for you, and you will eat the plants of the field. By the sweat of your brow you will eat your food until you return to the ground, since from it you were taken (Genesis 3:17b-19a).

Enjoy your work—for His glory and your delight.

Six days do your work, but on the seventh day do not work, so that your ox and your donkey may rest and the slave born in your household, and the alien as well, may be refreshed (Exodus 23:12).

Most of us don't understand the importance of work. We prefer rest and relaxation to a good day's work. The release of our potential requires that we acknowledge and move beyond the fallacies that characterize our view of work.

We are a rest-oriented society. We believe that holidays, vacation, and weekends are better than work days. This adoration of time free from work reflects our assumption that rest is to be preferred over work. This is a false assumption. Rest is not better than work.

When God created the world, He worked six days and rested one (see Gen. 2:2). He also instructed us to work six days and rest one (see Exod. 23:12). The result of our desire to work one day and rest six is evident in the boredom and unhappiness that plague our world.

Work always produces more personal growth and satisfaction than rest does. It stirs up your creative abilities and draws from the hidden store of your potential. If you are unfulfilled, you may be resting too much.

Sow your seed in the morning, and at evening let not your hands be idle, for you do not know which will succeed, whether this or that, or whether both will do equally well (Ecclesiastes 11:6).

A fallacy that affects our view of work is the assumption that retirement is the goal of work. You were not designed to retire. You came out of God, and God hasn't retired. He's been working ever since He spoke the invisible into the visible. Therefore, retirement is not part of His plan for your life. Because God created man by giving him an immortal spirit with eternal potential, God planned enough work to keep you busy forever. Oh, you may retire from a specific organization or job, but you can never retire from life and work. *The minute you quit working, you begin to die, because work is a necessary part of life.*

Have you ever met a retired person who was uncomfortable, bitter, rowdy, or senile? He (or she) became that way because he retired from work. The lack of work made him crazy because it took away his means of finding fulfillment.

May God deliver you from the spirit of retirement, because retirement is ungodly, unscriptural, and unbiblical. Retirement is foreign to God's plan for human beings.

God designed you to fulfill your potential for eternity.

His work will be shown for what it is, because the Day will bring it to light. It will be revealed with fire, and the fire will test the quality of each man's work. If what he has built survives, he will receive his reward (1 Corinthians 3:13-14).

---

*Y*ou cannot fulfill your purpose without work. Those who win the lottery often testify that they are more unhappy after they receive all that money than before. Why? Because they lost their reason for getting up in the morning.

Without purpose, life becomes meaningless. Life on "easy street" is not really easy because satisfaction requires effort. In fact, winning a million dollars could very well kill you if you stopped working. Oh, your body might live for a while, but your potential—the real you—would die from lack of use. The joy of life would be gone.

When you try to get something for nothing you miss the opportunity to find gratification, because effort is the key to satisfaction. *Benefits without work short-circuit fulfillment* because you usually have more appreciation for something you worked hard to get. You remember all you went through to obtain it, and from your remembering flows the impetus to treasure and care for the products of your labor.

Blessed are all who fear the Lord, who walk in His ways. You will eat the fruit of your labor; blessings and prosperity will be yours (Psalm 128:1-2).

The love of work is the secret to a productive life. Your very survival will be threatened as the various facets of your life fall apart from a lack of purpose. So crucial is your need to work that the absence of work is often the issue that underlies problems in interpersonal relationships.

Work is God's way to draw out your potential. Through work He opens the door into your inner storehouse and teaches you how to use your talents and abilities. That's why He is constantly giving you tasks that reveal more and more of the wealth that lies hidden within you. Little by little, He's chipping away at your storehouse of riches, trying to release all that He put in you.

You must refuse to allow the rest/retirement/ I-can-get-something-for-nothing mentality to rob you of your need to work. When you accept your responsibility to work and allow God to change your perceptions of work, you will see a difference in your life because God set work as a priority for personal gratification. Work is the master key to releasing your potential.

For we are God's fellow workers; you are God's field, God's building (1 Corinthians 3:9).

———— • ————

Have you ever noticed who God uses? God uses busy people. Truly God loves busy people because their busyness shows that they are willing to work. Jesus' preference for busy people is evident in His choice of four fishermen, who were preparing their nets, to be His first followers.

The priority Jesus put on work is also evident later in His ministry as He went through the towns and villages of Galilee and Judea, teaching in the synagogues and healing the sick. He saw there many people who were so helpless and harassed that He likened them to sheep without a shepherd. With compassion, He instructed His disciples to pray for workers to meet their needs:

Then [Jesus] *said to His disciples, "The harvest is plentiful but the workers* [laborers] *are few. Ask the Lord of the harvest, therefore, to send workers* [laborers] *into His harvest field"* (Matthew 9:37-38).

Jesus needed *workers*. He needed people who would give their best to bring others into the Kingdom of God. He told His disciples to pray that God would send somebody to work.

One who is slack in his work is brother to one who destroys (Proverbs 18:9).

When Jesus was on earth, He needed workers. He needed people who would give their best to bring others into the Kingdom of God. He told His disciples to pray that God would send somebody to work.

God hasn't changed. Work is still a priority for Him. Nor have the needs of our world changed. Helpless, harassed people still need what God stored in us for them.

But our human nature doesn't appreciate God's ways. We want results without the process. We seek promotion without responsibility. We desire pay without work. In order to participate in the creative power of the One who says, "I've given you the ability to produce, now work to see what you can do," you must cease to be a reluctant worker. You must choose to work, even if no one is standing over you, giving you the work, and making sure that you do it.

God expects us to understand our natural need to work. The Church, and the world at large, must recover God's principle of work because there can be no greatness without work. We must accept the truth that we need to work because God worked and He created us to work.

So on the seventh day He rested from all His work. And God blessed the seventh day and made it holy, because on it He rested from all the work of creating that He had done (Genesis 2:2b-3).

God set the priority of work when He called the invisible world into view. Before there was anything, there was God. Everything we now see existed first in God, but it was invisible. If God had done nothing to get started, the world we know would not exist. The universe would have stayed inside Him. But God chose to deliver His babies by *working*. He took His potential and, through effort, changed it from potential to experience.

God determined the number of stars and called them by name (see Ps. 147:4). He covered the sky with clouds, supplied the earth with rain, and made grass to grow on the hills (see Ps. 147:8). He formed the mountains by His power (see Ps. 65:6) and set the foundations of the earth (see Ps. 104:5). The moon marks the seasons by His decree and the sun sets at the appointed time (see Ps. 104:19). He savored the joy of seeing the wondrous beauty He had brought forth.

God saw all that He had made, and it was very good (Genesis 1:31a).

God's efforts in making the world are noteworthy. God didn't create the world by dreaming, wishing, or imagining. He created it by working. Indeed, God worked so hard that He had to rest.

So on the seventh day He rested from all His work. And God blessed the seventh day and made it holy, because on it He rested from all the work of creating that He had done (Genesis 2:2b-3).

Rest is needed after a long, laborious experience, not a tiny task that requires little effort. God's effort in creation was so extensive that He rested.

Too often we think that coming back to God means we don't have to work anymore. How wrong we are! God loves to work. He delights in pulling new things from His Omnipotent Self. He also requires you to work.

A curse on him who is lax in doing the Lord's work! A curse on him who keeps his sword from bloodshed! (Jeremiah 48:10)

After God finished creating the world and planting and organizing the Garden, He put Adam in the Garden and gave him work to do. Indeed, God had work on His mind before He even created human beings.

When the Lord God made the earth and the heavens—and no shrub of the field had yet appeared on the earth and no plant of the field had yet sprung up, for the Lord God had not sent rain on the earth and there was no man to work the ground, but streams came up from the earth and watered the whole surface of the ground— the Lord God formed the man from the dust of the ground and breathed into his nostrils the breath of life, and the man became a living being (Genesis 2:4b-7).

When God created Adam, He gave him dominion. Although we understand dominion to be sitting on a throne while others obey our every command, that is not God's intent. *God equates dominion with work. Every assignment God gave Adam required work.* Work was an essential part of Adam's life.

Nor did we eat anyone's food without paying for it. On the contrary, we worked night and day, laboring and toiling so that we would not be a burden to any of you (2 Thessalonians 3:8).

———————◆———————

When God created Adam, He gave him dominion. Adam had dominion over:

- Fish (water)
- Birds (air)
- Living creatures (land)

This dominion meant that Adam had to work. Work was an essential part of Adam's life.

The same is true for you. God created you to work. He didn't create you to rest or retire or go on vacation. He didn't create you to punch a time card or to stand under the eagle eye of a boss or supervisor. He gave you birth to experience fulfillment by completing tasks through effort.

Work is a gift from God. Every assignment God has ever given required work. Noah worked to build the ark (see Gen. 6). Joseph worked to provide for the Egyptians during a seven-year famine (see Gen. 41:41). Solomon worked to build the Temple (see 2 Chron. 2-4). As each accomplished what God asked of him, he fulfilled God's purpose for his life. His willingness to do the work God gave him blessed himself and others.

All hard work brings a profit... (Proverbs 14:23).

———————

Work is honorable. God designed you to meet the needs of your life through work. When you refuse to work, you deny yourself the opportunity to fulfill your purpose, because God created you to act like He acts, and God worked. The release of your potential demands that you admit that you need work.

The plans of the diligent lead to profit... (Proverbs 21:5).

Make it your ambition to lead a quiet life, to mind your own business and to **work** *with your hands...so that your daily life may win the respect of outsiders and so that* **you will not be dependent on anybody** (1 Thessalonians 4:11-12).

Work profits the worker by allowing him to meet his financial responsibilities. The apostle Paul provided for his own needs by making tents (see 1 Thess. 2:6-9). He did not rely on the provisions of others, but whenever possible, worked for his living.

The same is required of you. Don't become a burden on others. Work to provide for yourself and your family. Settle down and get a job. Put your roots down and do not allow yourself to be easily deterred from your responsibilities. God gave you work to earn the bread you eat.

Do your best to present yourself to God as one approved, a workman who does not need to be ashamed and who correctly handles the Word of truth (2 Timothy 2:15).

Work profits the worker…

…by revealing potential. Although all work brings profit, the reward is not always a financial one. God does not lie. Even if no one ever pays you, your work profits you because you discover what you can do.

…by unveiling the blessings of work.

Work is much more important than honor because it brings the learning that releases your talents, abilities, and capabilities. It is also more valuable than a paycheck. When you stop working for money, you'll discover the blessing of work.

…by giving the opportunity to rejoice in achievement.

A commitment to work will also permit you to develop a perspective that rejoices in achievement more than pay. *If you want to be promoted, get busy. Become productive.*

…by building self-esteem.

Finally, work profits you by enhancing your self-esteem. If you feel worthless, find some work. Get busy. When you have something to do, your ability to feel good about yourself can change overnight. Work keeps you healthy, physically and emotionally.

...I have never seen the righteous forsaken or their children begging bread. They are always generous and lend freely; their children will be blessed (Psalm 37:25-26).

Work affords the opportunity to help others. Indeed, the Gospel of Matthew records a parable in which our willingness to help meet the needs of others is the basis on which our faithfulness or unfaithfulness to Christ is judged (see Matt. 25:31-46). The apostle Paul notes the benefits of sharing when he commends the Corinthian church for their willingness to help sister churches in need (see 2 Cor. 8-9). He advises them to give generously, not grudgingly, with the promise that what they give and more will be returned to them:

Remember this: Whoever sows sparingly will also reap sparingly, and whoever sows generously will also reap generously. Each man should give what he has decided in his heart to give, not reluctantly or under compulsion, for God loves a cheerful giver.... Now He who supplies seed to the sower and bread for food will also supply and increase your store of seed and will enlarge the harvest of your righteousness. You will be made rich in every way so that you can be generous on every occasion... (2 Corinthians 9:6-7,10-11a).

...their children will be blessed (Psalm 37:26b).

———◆·◆———

If I were to ask you to describe a thief, you would probably talk about someone who entered your home and took your possessions. This is certainly a legitimate definition, but the thief doesn't always have to sneak in and out to take what isn't his.

Many of us go to work and steal from our bosses. We come to work late, take extra long lunch hours, and go home early. Or we take home the pencils, paper, pens, and paper clips that belong to the company, we make private copies on the boss's copy machine, and we conduct personal business on company time. These actions are no better than those of a thief who enters your home and takes your possessions because both result in the loss of goods that someone else worked to provide.

In an even broader sense, a thief is anyone who relies on the productiveness of another to provide for his needs because he is too lazy to meet them himself. If you are able to work and you're not working, you are stealing from those who are working. *Taking the benefits of work without participating in the effort is theft.*

He who has been stealing must steal no longer, but must work, doing something useful with his own hands... (Ephesians 4:28).

If you are able to work and you're not working, you are stealing from those who are working. You are pregnant with babies that need to be born. You have talents, abilities, and capabilities that God wants you to share with the world. But you will never see them unless you begin to understand God's definition of work and His purpose for giving you the opportunity to share His creative powers. Your potential is dying while you are sitting around doing nothing.

If you steal something, you don't stop and look at it. Instead of admiring your efforts, you worry about who's going to take your things from you. Or you are so busy seeing how little work you can do without being caught that you have accomplished nothing at the end of the day that merits the pride of accomplishment. *The absence of work is stealing. Likewise, the cure for stealing is work—doing something useful with your hands.*

Usefulness is more than a job. Usefulness recognizes the accomplishments of others and tries to complement them.

Even when we were with you, we gave you this rule: "If a man will not work, he shall not eat" (2 Thessalonians 3:10).

⎯⎯●⎯⎯

Sitting around is no more acceptable to God than taking what does not belong to you. You rob yourself and others when you are lazy. Like any theft, laziness carries many penalties.

The first of these is *hunger*:

The sluggard craves and gets nothing, but the desires of the diligent are fully satisfied (Proverbs 13:4).

Laziness brings on deep sleep, and the shiftless man goes hungry (Proverbs 19:15).

A second penalty of laziness is *isolation* and *shame*:

In the name of the Lord Jesus Christ, we command you, brothers, to keep away from every brother who is idle....Do not associate with him, in order that he may feel ashamed (2 Thessalonians 3:6,14b).

A poor man is shunned by all his relatives—how much more do his friends avoid him! (Proverbs 19:7a)

A third penalty of laziness is *others' reluctance to take you seriously*, because lazy people always have an excuse why they aren't working.

The sluggard says, "There is a lion outside!" or, "I will be murdered in the streets!" (Proverbs 22:13)

Do you see a man skilled in his work? He will serve before kings; he will not serve before obscure men (Proverbs 22:29).

———•———

Like any theft, laziness carries many penalties.

A fourth penalty of laziness is *lost opportunities for advancement* because jealousy and over concern for the progress of others prevents you from doing your work. (See Proverbs 27:23-24.)

A fifth penalty of laziness is *the inability to see your own need to get up and work.* (See Proverbs 26:16.)

A sixth penalty of laziness is an increasing *loss of ambition:*

The sluggard buries his hand in the dish; he is too lazy to bring it back to his mouth (Proverbs 26:15).

A seventh penalty of laziness is the *desire to sleep:*

As a door turns on its hinges, so a sluggard turns on his bed (Proverbs 26:14).

An eighth penalty of laziness is *the inability to take pride in what you have accomplished* because you haven't accomplished anything. (See Proverbs 12:27.)

A ninth penalty of laziness is *slavery*:

Diligent hands will rule, but laziness ends in slave labor (Proverbs 12:24).

An tenth penalty of laziness, and the most severe, is *poverty*. Poverty is the cumulative result of all the other penalties. (See Proverbs 14:23.)

Go to the ant, you sluggard; consider its ways and be wise! It has no commander, no overseer or ruler, yet it stores its provisions in summer and gathers its food at harvest (Proverbs 6:6-8).

The most severe penalty of laziness is poverty. Poverty is the cumulative result of all the other penalties we looked at. (See Proverbs 14:23; 6:9-11.)

A sluggard is a lazy bum—my mother used to call them "grassy bellies." When I was young I did not understand what my mom meant. But one day when I was sitting in the library at the university I realized that Mom called sluggards grassy bellies because they lay on their bellies long enough for grass to grow on them. The Greek word for *poor*, as used by Jesus, is *poucos*, which means "nonproductivity." That's what poverty is. To be poor doesn't mean you don't *have* anything. It means you aren't *doing* anything.

Poverty is cured by hard work. If you don't work you will end up begging. Or you'll become a slave to your boss because you refuse to work for your own satisfaction in completing the job and wait for him to force you to work.

Work is God's path to an abundant, fulfilling life that reveals the wealth of your potential.

243

Share with God's people who are in need.
Practice hospitality (Romans 12:13).

The power of productivity is evident today in the influence of labor unions. Because unions control the workers, who control the productivity, they can cripple a country, destroy an economy, and control a government. And once you control productivity, you control wealth.

Do you know how countries measure their strength and wealth? They measure it not by the money they have in their treasury, but by their GNP, which means gross national product. Thus, the relative strength or weakness of a country is measured by the level of employment and productivity. The power of productivity is work.

When people decide they aren't going to work, the back of a nation is broken. Thus, the demise of world-class companies is not the fault of the board or the president. The cause rests with the little guys who push wheels on a plane or weld car parts together. Our countries suffer when our people refuse to work, and work well. We must change our attitudes toward work.

Our hope comes in rediscovering God's definition of work and the benefits He intends work to bring to our lives.

*Why spend money on what is not bread,
and your labor on what does not satisfy?
Listen, listen to me, and eat what is good,
and your soul will delight in the richest of
fare* (Isaiah 55:2).

Our definition of work and God's are very differ-ent. Work is not the same as a job. Work releas-es potential; a job provides a paycheck. While you may work at your job, work does not always result in a financial reward. Work arises out of a desire to contribute to the world's wealth and well-being by giving of yourself.

Frequently we make work overly sophisticated. We need to get labor back into work. We need to *labor* in the office, not just go to the office. God didn't say, "Six days you shall go to your job," but "six days you shall work." Until we change our attitude toward work we will not obey this commandment.

Jesus commanded us to pray for *laborers*. This term is also used to describe the process of a woman in childbearing. All are necessary for the manifesta-tion of a child. This process is the same for all humanity. Labor delivers!

Diligent hands will rule, but laziness ends in slave labor (Proverbs 12:24).

Jesus worked while He was on the earth. He gave sight to the blind and hearing to the deaf. He preached the good news of God's coming Kingdom and welcomed sinners into God's family. Jesus knew that He had been sent to redeem a suffering, dying world. He accepted the task God gave Him and worked to change the course of history. Indeed, the results of His work were the clues Jesus pointed to when He was questioned whether He was the One to be sent from God.

Jesus said to them, "My Father is always at His work to this very day, and I, too, am working" (John 5:17).

You have a similar responsibility to release the strength and energy God gave you for the good of the world. You can accomplish this through work. Through work you can do and become all that God intended for your life.

Potential is what you have. Work is what you do. What you do with what you have makes the difference between a life of strength and energy, and a life of weakness and defeat. God gives you work to activate your power. Through work you become what you are.

And we pray this in order that you may live a life worthy of the Lord and may please Him in every way: bearing fruit in every good work, growing in the knowledge of God (Colossians 1:10).

A fantasy is a dream without labor. It is also a vision without a mission. When God gives the potential for something, He also demands that it be worked out. The story of Abraham is a good example of this principle (see Gen. 13:14-17).

One day when God and Abraham were on top of a mountain, God told Abraham that He would give him everything as far as he could see to the north, south, east, and west. But the promise would not be possession without effort. The same is true for you. Every time God gives you a promise, He also gives you the command to work to receive what He has promised. God doesn't just deliver like Santa Claus. You have to fight to get what is yours.

Every job, no matter how much you dislike it, is working for you. If you can educate yourself to work no matter what the conditions are, you will learn discipline, because the work is more important than the conditions.

Without work, all you have is potential.

So we rebuilt the wall till all of it reached half its height, for the people worked with all their heart (Nehemiah 4:6).

When God wanted a place to live, He could have created a magnificent dwelling by speaking it into place. But He chose to have man build the house for Him. Thus, God instructed Moses to gather offerings for the Tabernacle and to employ skilled craftsmen to create its various parts. After Moses had collected the materials and the workers, the work began. Silversmiths, goldsmiths, carpenters, glass cutters, weavers, embroiderers, and gem cutters all contributed their *skills* until the dwelling place of God was completed. Then the Lord, through His presence in the cloud by day and the pillar of fire by night, entered and filled the Tabernacle *they had prepared.*

God has given you a wealth of skills, talents, and abilities. Work is the means to discovering those resources. Persistent, consistent effort polishes the gems within you, making your life a suitable dwelling place for our holy God. It activates your potential and enables you to share your expertise and proficiency. The release of your gifts will benefit the world for generations to come.

As God's fellow workers we urge you not to receive God's grace in vain (2 Corinthians 6:1).

————————

Work provides the means to activate the knowledge you gained through the study of the other keys to your potential. It takes you from knowing that you must live by faith to acting on what you know. Knowledge is not profitable until it is translated into action. Work is the translator God has provided.

Work is part of your design. If you're not working, you're not fulfilling your purpose. In God's system, everyone *needs* to work. *You* need to work. Your ability to dominate and subdue the earth is related to the effort you put forth to accomplish the tasks God gives you. If you refuse to work, your potential to express God's image and to bear fruit are sealed inside you, dormant and useless. Without labor there is no fruit, and the blessings God wants to give you are forfeited. Your refusal to work destroys the possibilities you possess to cooperate with God's work of creation.

People tend to gravitate to those who think and act like they do. This is certainly true of those who avoid work. Lazy people don't like to be in the company of diligent people because their non-productivity is readily visible.

The plans of the diligent lead to profit as surely as haste leads to poverty (Proverbs 21:5).

Do you want to be a lawyer, a doctor, a teacher, a carpenter, a police officer, a minister, a secretary, an accountant, or a politician? Put some work behind that dream. Burn the midnight oil and study. Make the acquaintance of a person who is working in your chosen field and work with him or her to learn the trade, business, or profession. The completion of your plans is related to your willingness to work, as is your prosperity. Likewise, *the release of your potential is dependent upon your expenditure of the necessary effort to change your thoughts into visible realities. Work of your own initiative. Don't wait for life to force you to work.*

Work is the key to your personal progress, productivity, and fulfillment. Without work you can accomplish nothing. God assigns you work so you can release your possibilities and abilities by putting forth the effort to accomplish each task.

Accept today God's gracious gift of work. Refuse to allow a pessimistic attitude toward work to rob you of your potential.

The disciples, each according to his ability, decided to provide help for the brothers living in Judea (Acts 11:29).

One of the most beautiful sounds to ever enter the human ear is the first cry of a newborn baby—the sound of life! Millions of people over the years have experienced much joy, elation, celebration, and relief at this sound. Yet, a newborn's cry also signals the arrival of responsibility. Not only do the parents have the responsibility for the new infant but the child himself becomes accountable for the awesome potential he possesses at birth.

All human beings come to this world pregnant with potential. Each person, like a computer, has a tremendous capacity to compute, analyze, assimilate, compare, and produce. But this ability is useless until it is programmed and demands are made on it. Your potential, ability, and natural talent were given by Divine Providence for the purpose of preparing the next generation to fulfill its potential. No one comes to this earth empty.

The fact that you were born is evidence that you possess something that can benefit the world. No matter what you have done or accomplished, there is still much more inside you that needs to be released. Only you can release it.

*The Lord God took the man and put him in
the Garden of Eden to work it and take care
of it* (Genesis 2:15).

I am convinced that life was designed to create
environments that make demands on our potential. Without these demands our potential would lie
dormant. This thought is reflected in the saying,
"Necessity is the mother of invention." How true!
Most of us respond to life creatively and innovative-
ly only when circumstances *demand* that response.
The many technological, medical, and social break-
throughs that have been achieved because problems
or circumstances demanded a response vividly illus-
trate this truth. The Book of Genesis also clearly
reveals this principle in the account of man's first
encounter with creation in the Garden of Eden.

Man, as God first created him, was 100 percent
unreleased potential. He was an adult with full capabilities, talents, and gifts. His physical, mental, intellectual, emotional, and spiritual powers were fully
developed. But man's powers and abilities were
totally unused, untapped, unmanifested, unchal-
lenged, and unemployed.

Your potential is released when demands are
placed on you to fulfill an assignment in God's
greater purpose for your life. This is why *work* is
called *employment*—it employs your abilities for the
purpose of manifesting your potential.

For I testify that they gave as much as they were able, and even beyond their ability. Entirely on their own (2 Corinthians 8:3).

God's command to work required Adam to use his physical potential. Likewise, God's commands to *cultivate the garden* and to *name the animals* activated his intellectual, mental, and creative potential. The demands God makes on you accomplish the same thing in your life. You will never know the extent of your potential until you give it something to do. The greatest tragedy in your life will not be your death, but what dies with you at death. What a shame to waste what God gave you to use.

Have you ever noticed the deep peace and contentment that come over you when you fulfill a responsibility? The joy and elation that fill you at such times are the fruit of achievement.

The experience of fulfillment is directly related to this principle of *finishing*. An old Chinese proverb says: "The end of a thing is greater than its beginning." In other words, finishing is more important than starting. The beginning of a task may bring a degree of anxiety and apprehension, but the completing of a task usually yields a sense of relief, joy, and fulfillment.

For I am already being poured out like a drink offering, and the time has come for my departure. I have fought a good fight, I have finished my race, I have kept the faith (2 Timothy 4:6-7).

Paul faced death with complete confidence and peace because he knew that he had fulfilled God's purpose for his life. When he spoke of being "poured out," which suggests emptying some contents from oneself, he pointed to an accurate and important concept that must be understood by all who would release their potential.

You, like Paul and our Lord Jesus Christ, were born for a purpose. The ability to fulfill that purpose resides deep inside you screaming to be released. Perhaps you yearn to write books, compose songs, scribe poetry, obtain an academic degree, paint on canvas, play music, open a business, serve in a political, civic, or spiritual organization, visit other countries, or develop an invention. Think how long you've carried your dream. Recall how many times you have postponed satisfying your desire. Count the many times you began to realize your goal only to quit.

What steps can you take now to achieve this dream?

A good man leaves an inheritance for his children's children... (Proverbs 13:22).

———————◆———————

*G*od designed everything not only to reproduce itself but also to transfer and transmit its life and treasure to the next generation. Consider the seed of a tree. Every seed comes into this world to deliver a tree, which in turn delivers more seeds, which produce more trees, and on and on it goes. All aspects of creation possess this generational principle.

If all the seeds in the world withheld the potential of the trees within them, a natural tragedy would be the result. The bees would suffer, the birds would die, and the animals would starve to death. The genocide of man would also occur as oxygen disappeared from the atmosphere. All this would occur because one element in nature refused to fulfill the purpose for which it was created.

No man is born to live or die unto himself. Tragedy strikes whenever a person fails to die empty. God gave you the wealth of your potential— your abilities, gifts, talents, energies, creativity, ideas, aspirations, and desires—for the blessing of future generations. You bear the responsibility to activate, release, and deposit them. This generational principle of God, the Father of creation, is crucial to your full appreciation of the principle of potential.

Consider well her ramparts, view her citadels, that you may tell of them to the next generation (Psalm 48:13).

God gave you the wealth of your potential—your abilities, gifts, talents, energies, creativity, ideas, aspirations, and desires—for the blessing of future generations. You bear the responsibility to activate, release, and deposit them. This generational principle of God, the Father of creation, is crucial to your full appreciation of the principle of potential. Tragedy strikes whenever a person fails to die empty.

I wonder how many hundreds of people—perhaps thousands or millions—were born or are yet to be born who need to benefit from the books you have thus far neglected to write, the songs you have failed to compose, or the invention you have continued to postpone. Perhaps there are millions who need the ministry you have yet to begin or the business venture you have not yet started.

The next generation needs the treasure of your potential. You must not die unfinished and let the grave steal the gems of the future. Deliver your potential to inspire the children of our world to release theirs.

Give, and it will be given to you. A good measure, pressed down, shaken together and running over, will be poured into your lap. For with the measure you use, it will be measured to you (Luke 6:38).

History reveals the truth that any people who are robbed by oppression, suppression, depression, and subjugation of the opportunity to activate, release, and maximize their potential suffer from the loss of generational thinking. Their oppression forces them to think in terms of self-preservation and personal security with little thought for posterity and the future. This mentality pervades many Third World nations today, manifesting itself in an attitude and a lifestyle that encourages *immediate gratification at the expense of the future*. This mind-set ultimately leads to fear, distrust, suspicion, and resentment among members of the same ethnic community.

This lack of generational consciousness traps individuals in a cycle of self-maintenance and retards creativity, inspiration, and innovation. Consequently, the release of the tremendous abilities that lie within every individual is forfeited. Third World people everywhere must be delivered from this mentality. It is essential that they understand the responsibility they have to their children and their children's children. *Until a man can see beyond his own loins, the future is in danger.*

By faith Abraham, even though he was past age—and Sarah herself was barren—was enabled to become a father because he considered Him faithful who had made the promise (Hebrews 11:11).

It was 4 o'clock on a cold, wet, winter morning. The small town appeared to be drugged as farmers, storekeepers, and street sweepers dragged themselves to their places of business. Suddenly, a young boy about 12 years of age appeared, happily skipping along as he clutched an old cello case.

Pablo Casals's interest in and commitment to music at such an early age inspired even his teacher. Through the years, his work, accomplishments, and achievements have been testimonies of greatness that stand worthy of emulation.

After a lifetime of distinguished achievements, Pablo Casals, at age 85, continued to rise early and practice his cello. When asked why he practiced five hours a day, he replied, "Because I think I'm getting better."

Pablo Casals reminds us of the character of men and women such as Abraham, who accepted the vision of a baby destined to change the world and believed it would come to pass.

I have worked much harder, been in prison more frequently, been flogged more severely, and been exposed to death again and again (2 Corinthians 11:23b).

Great minds and souls, knowing always that what they have done must never be confused with what they can yet do, never settle for great work. The concept of retirement is a great myth that traps the untapped potential buried in millions of talented, gifted, and valuable individuals. This Western concept has caused many great men and women to settle for the average and to succumb to the mediocrity of the socially accepted standards of success. However, all individuals throughout history who have left their footprints in the sands of destiny were driven by a passion greater than the desire for personal comfort.

Abraham accepted the vision of a baby destined to change the world and believed it would come to pass. Abraham saw the fruit of his faith when he was 100 years old. Moses changed careers mid-life from a sheep-herding fugitive to a deliverer and national leader of over 3 million people. David, the great king of Israel, worked in the twilight of his many years of excellent leadership to make plans for the construction of a magnificent temple that was eventually built by his son Solomon.

I have fought the good fight, I have finished the race, I have kept the faith (2 Timothy 4:7).

———•———

Paul, the unrivaled apostle of the Church, after many years of tremendous hardship, wrote a brief description of his challenges in a letter to the church at Corinth. He stated:

I have worked much harder, been in prison more frequently, been flogged more severely, and been exposed to death again and again. Five times I received from the Jews the forty lashes minus one. Three times I was beaten with rods, once I was stoned, three times I was shipwrecked, I spent a night and a day in the open sea, I have been constantly on the move. I have been in danger from rivers, in danger from bandits, in danger from my own countrymen, in danger from Gentiles; in danger in the city, in danger in the country, in danger at sea; and in danger from false brothers. I have labored and toiled and have often gone without sleep; I have known hunger and thirst and have often gone without food; I have been cold and naked (2 Corinthians 11:23b-27).

Then this great leader exclaims: *"Who is weak, and I do not feel weak?"* (2 Cor. 11:29a).

"This is my blood of the covenant, which is poured out for many," He said to them (Mark 14:24).

———•———

Paul's perception of life, and the responsibility of each of us to maximize life to its fullest potential, is expressed in his final letter to Timothy. To this favorite young student, he wrote:

For I am already being poured out like a drink offering, and the time has come for my departure. I have fought the good fight, I have finished the race, I have kept the faith (2 Timothy 4:6-7).

Paul likened his life to the ceremonial drink offering administered by the priest in the Old Testament rituals of the Temple, in which the priest filled a cup with wine and ceremonially poured it out at intervals in the service until the cup was completely empty.

Your life is like a cup of drink served to the world by our great Creator. The drink is the awesome, untapped, valuable, destiny-filled treasure, gifts, and talents of potential buried within you. Every minute, day, month, and year is an interval of opportunity provided by God for the pouring out of another portion of yourself until you have exposed all His precious treasure that makes you unique. This is called *maximum living*.

Arise, shine, for your light has come, and the glory of the Lord rises upon you (Isaiah 60:1).

What does it mean to maximize? The word *maximum* may be defined as "supreme, greatest, highest, and ultimate." It is synonymous with such concepts as pinnacle, preeminence, culmination, apex, peak, and summit. It implies the highest degree possible. Just a brief look at these concepts immediately convicts us of the many opportunities we have abused and forfeited because we have failed or have refused to give our all.

Therefore, to *maximize* is to express, expose, experience, and execute all the hidden, God-given abilities, talents, gifts, and potential through God's vision breathed in our souls to fulfill His purpose for our lives on earth.

Anything less than maximum is mediocrity. Mediocrity is the spirit of the average, the anthem of the norm, and the heartbeat of the ordinary. Mediocrity is so common and pervasive that those who are labeled as genius or exceptional have to do only a little extra.

Why do so many of us settle for mediocrity? The answer is found in what I call the curse of comparison.

We do not dare to classify or compare ourselves with some who commend themselves. When they measure themselves by themselves and compare themselves with themselves, they are not wise (2 Corinthians 10:12).

The autobahn is a network of roads, without speed restrictions, that crisscross Germany and many other neighboring countries. One day as we were traveling from a city in northern Germany to the south, my host asked if I would like to experience driving without a speed limitation.

At first I was excited, thrilled, and anxious as I felt adrenaline rush through my entire body. As the pressure of my foot accelerated the engine, I felt the thrill of a car traveling at 115 mph. I was the king of the road, master of the highway.

Suddenly, a Mercedes-Benz cruised past me at 150 mph, seemingly coming out of nowhere. Instantly, I felt like I was standing still. My host turned to me and said with a chuckle, "So you see, you are not traveling as fast as you can, but only as fast as you will."

I learned three lessons that have become the foundations of my thinking concerning success and effective living: the principle of *capacity*, the principle of *comparison*, and the principle of *experience*.

I know that when I come to you, I will come in the full measure of the blessing of Christ (Romans 15:29).

The true capacity of a product is determined not by the user but the manufacturer. If an automobile is built with the capacity to travel at 180 mph, its full potential was determined by the manufacturer. The true potential of the car is not affected by my opinion of its ability or by my previous experience with driving. Whether or not I use the full capacity of the car's engine does not reduce its potential capacity.

The same principle applies to your life. God created you like He did everything else, with the capacity to fulfill your purpose. Therefore, your true capacity is not limited, reduced, or altered by the opinion of others or your previous experience. You are capable of attaining the total aptitude given to you by your Creator to fulfill His purpose for your life. Therefore, *the key to maximizing your full potential is to discover the purpose or reason for your life and commit to its fulfillment at all cost.*

No human has the right or the ability to fully determine or measure the capacity of the potential you possess.

The Lord does not look at the things man looks at. Man looks at the outward appearance, but the Lord looks at the heart (1 Samuel 16:7b).

————◆————

When I was driving on the autobahn in Europe, I was in a position of great success and achievement if I compared myself to the drivers I overtook. Yet, even though for awhile I was leading all the others, I was still not operating at *my car's* full potential. The car's true capacity was 180 mph, and I was traveling at 115 mph. When I compared my car's performance to all the others, I was leading the pack; I could have been considered a success in their eyes because I was traveling faster than all of them. When I compared my car's performance to its true capacity, however, I was not truly successful because I was traveling below the maximum speed built into the car by the manufacturer.

The lesson here is that true success is not measured by how much you have done or accomplished compared to what others have done or accomplished; *true success is what you have done compared to what you could have done.*

If anyone thinks he is something when he is nothing, he deceives himself. Each one should test his own actions. Then he can take pride in himself, without comparing himself to somebody else, for each one should carry his own load [responsibility] (Galatians 6:3-5).

From the early years of childhood, we are compared to our sisters and brothers, the neighbor's children, or some other person. This comparative spirit continues on into our teen and adult years, developing into a sophisticated dehumanizing state of competition. The result is traumatizing because we spend most of our lives trying to compete with others, comparing our achievements with those of our peers, and attempting to live up to their standards of acceptance.

If we compete with ourselves and not with others, then it does not matter who is behind us or ahead of us; our goal is to become and achieve all we are capable of being and doing, and this becomes the measure of our satisfaction.

The apostle Paul, the great leader of the Church, commented on this critical issue in Second Corinthians 10:12-13. His statements strongly admonish us not to compete with others or to compare our talents with their abilities or potential, since we are responsible only for our potential, not theirs.

*If we claim to have fellowship with Him yet
walk in the darkness, we lie and do not live
by the truth* (1 John 1:6).

Experience may be defined as "the observation of
facts as a source of knowledge and skill gained
by contact with facts and events." By its very nature,
experience is a product of the past and is, therefore,
limited to and controlled by previous exposure. In
spite of the fact that experience may be valuable for
making decisions and judgments concerning the
future, it is important to know that any significant
measurement of growth, development, expansion, or
advancement will require experience to submit to
the substance of the unknown through faith.

Experience is given not to determine the limits
of our lives, but to create a better life for us.
Experience is a tool to be used! My experience with
driving over the years has conditioned me to drive a
car monitored by the speed limits established by the
society in which I live. Therefore, my driving capacity has become subject to the accepted norms of 45-
60 mph. However, the fact that I have driven my car
at 45-60 mph for over 25 years does not cancel the
automobile's capacity to travel at 100-180 mph.

You have potential within you that goes beyond
your past experience of what you can do.

By faith Enoch was taken from this life, so that he did not experience death; he could not be found, because God had taken him away. For before he was taken, he was commended as one who pleased God (Hebrews 11:5).

This world is filled with millions of individuals who are capable of traveling at a maximum capacity of 180 mph, but they have settled for 55 mph. Because they have overtaken some folks or have exceeded the expectations of a few others, they have compared their lives to these persons and have accepted mediocrity as excellence.

Experience is given not to determine the limits of our lives, but to create a better life for us.

At any point in our lives, we are the sum total of all the decisions we have made, the people we have met, the exposure we have had, and the facts we have learned. In essence, every human is a walking history book. We must be careful not to allow our past to determine the quality of our future. Instead, we must use our experience to help us make better decisions, always guarding against the possibility that it may limit our decisions. *Remember, your ability is never limited to your experience.*

For it is God who works in you to will and to act according to His good purpose (Philippians 2:13).

———◆———

One of life's great tragedies is that the majority of the world's population is composed of individuals who have negotiated an agreement with mediocrity, signed a contract with the average, and pledged allegiance to the ordinary. God expects more!

The urge to accomplish great things and engage in significant endeavors is the germ of purpose planted by God in the heart of man. Why then do we settle for so little? Why do we abandon our dreams and deny our purpose? Why do we live below our privilege, buried in the cemetery of wishful thinking and empty regrets?

As we have seen, one reason we fail to progress in fulfilling our purpose is satisfaction with our present measure of success. The belief that we have arrived is the deterrent that keeps us from getting to our destination. A second part of the answer of why we settle for mediocrity is that we have accepted the present state of our lives as the best we can do under the circumstances.

Equip you with everything good for doing His will, and may He work in us what is pleasing to Him, through Jesus Christ, to whom be glory for ever and ever. Amen (Hebrews 13:21).

One reason we fail to progress in fulfilling our purpose is that we have accepted the present state of our lives as the best we can do under the circumstances. This concept, "under the circumstances," serves to imprison us and to immobilize our God-given ambition because too many of us have surrendered to the status quo and have become prisoners of the war for our minds. We forget that "circumstances" are simply temporary arrangements of life to which we are all exposed.

We overlook or disregard the fact that these circumstances are designed to identify, expose, develop, refine, and maximize our true potential. It's not what happens to us that matters, but what we do with what happens. Much of the time we are not responsible for our circumstances, but we are always responsible for our response to those circumstances. *One key to maximizing your potential is to become dissatisfied with the circumstances that restrict, limit, and stifle your potential.*

Like an eagle that stirs up its nest and hovers over its young, that spreads its wings to catch them and carries them on its pinions. The Lord alone [leads you] (Deuteronomy 32:11-12a).

Remember, *we cannot become what we were born to be by remaining what we are.* Just as the mother eagle removes the comforts of her feathery nest to "disturb" the young eaglets into flying, so our Creator moves us beyond our comfort zones so that we are forced to fly. Without this stirring, most of us would never fly.

An eagle that doesn't fly cannot fulfill its purpose. Likewise, your life will lack purpose and focus until you discover your wings. This discovery will require both wisdom and courage because the thrill of flying always begins with the fear of falling. Yet you are not left alone to find your wings because God, through the prophet Moses, promises to undertake for you.

Indeed, the greatest gift God can offer you is to push you into a crisis of temporary discomfort that requires you to try your wings. This pushing into crisis is His supreme act of love, akin to that of a mother eagle that pushes her young from the nest to force them to fly.

Set His seal of ownership on us, and put His Spirit in our hearts as a deposit, guaranteeing what is to come (2 Corinthians 1:22).

Paul refers to this hidden wealth within as *"treasure in jars of clay"* (2 Cor. 4:7). The jar may not look like much, but the treasure inside it is valuable and priceless. In other words, *what people see when they look at you is not who you truly are. You can become much more than you now are.*

Who would have thought that Saul of Tarsus, a fervent Jew who vigorously opposed the followers of Jesus, would become Paul the apostle, the greatest missionary the Church has ever known? Certainly not the Christians he persecuted—they did not expect anything good from him (see Acts 9:20-21)—nor Saul himself. Not in his wildest imaginings would he have seen himself as a servant of the One he despised. Yet, Saul contained a dormant wealth that was not evident under the outer trappings of his misguided religious fervor.

That same wealth is present in you. You are capable of more than others expect of you—even beyond your own most extravagant dreams. Unexposed, dormant potential rests beneath the surface of your daily existence, waiting to be discovered and released.

*May you be blessed by the Lord, the Maker
of Heaven and earth* (Psalm 115:15).

If you are going to move from who you now are to
who God created you to be, you must seek to
understand the nature of God's original design for
you, before sin ravaged your life. That understanding is not available to you unless you become reconnected with God, your Creator. *You must know God,
your Source, if you want to experience a satisfying,
abundant life.*

Saul of Tarsus met his Source on the road to
Damascus when Jesus Christ spoke to him from a
bright light that left him blind. For three days he
waited before God. God sent Ananias to place his
hands on Saul to restore his sight and to bring the
Holy Spirit into his life.

What a change! Few of us will experience a
change as dramatic, but a change just as radical—
from being self-centered to God-centered—must
occur in all who would discover and use their full
potential. You must have a life-changing encounter
with the One who made you if you want to become
who you were created to be.

[I] live by faith, not by sight (2 Corinthians 5:7).

———•———

No builder can successfully restore a house unless he first knows the specifications determined by the builder and the features provided by the original blueprints. A shower, for example, may fulfill part of the designer's intent for the bathroom, but it cannot match all the functions of a bathtub. Thus, installing a shower in place of a tub would change not only the room's appearance but also its ability to provide the intended functions that were built into the original design.

We are designed to live by faith. The Book of Hebrews defines faith as *"being sure of what we hope for and certain of what we do not see"* (Heb. 11:1). God is not influenced by outward appearances; neither is His power diminished by seemingly impossible obstacles.

Your ability to unleash your potential is tied to your willingness to consistently live from God's perspective, which saw Paul the apostle in Saul the murderer. He created you to share His viewpoint. If you allow the obstacles that clutter your path and the expectations of others to discourage you and to send you on time- and energy-consuming detours, your God-given talents and abilities will be wasted.

...God, who set me apart from birth and called me by His grace, was pleased to reveal His Son in me so that I might preach Him among the Gentiles... (Galatians 1:15-16).

To fully release your potential, you must discover your corporate and specific reason for existence and the accompanying assignment. One of the first tasks of a builder who wants to restore an old house is to determine the purpose for each room. Although this purpose may not be immediately evident, the rebuilding cannot accurately and effectively duplicate the original building if the purpose for each room is not established.

In a similar manner, you cannot effectively release your potential if you do not discover God's purpose for giving you life. Your potential and your purpose are perfectly related because God never requires you to do or be something that is not part of His purpose. Likewise, He never requires something of you that He did not provide for when He created you. Your potential enables you to fulfill your purpose, and your purpose reveals the potential hidden within you.

Success without an understanding of purpose is meaningless. He alone knows why He created you with the specific combination of personality, abilities, and dreams that make you the unique individual you are.

Command those who are rich in this present world not to be arrogant nor to put their hope in wealth, which is so uncertain, but to put their hope in God, who richly provides us with everything for our enjoyment (1 Timothy 6:17).

Provisions are given for the fulfillment of vision. Every builder, before he starts a project, both estimates what materials he will need to complete the job and determines what resources are available to him. God functions in a similar manner. As He forms and fashions each person for a specific purpose, He also provides the necessary resources to accomplish His plans.

The apostle Paul knew that God had given him certain resources to help him fulfill his purpose and release his potential. Varied in nature and use, these resources included his tent-making skills, his Roman citizenship, his Jewish education and upbringing, and, most importantly, his faith in Jesus Christ and his confidence that God, through the Spirit, had given him a message for the world. (See Romans 15:15-19.)

Paul was careful, however, to view these resources only as tools given by God to accomplish His plans. Therefore, he always treated his resources as being less important than the One who gave them.

"I [the Lord] will live with them and walk among them, and I will be their God, and they will be My people. Therefore come out from them and be separate, says the Lord. Touch no unclean thing, and I will receive you. I will be a Father to you..."
...let us purify ourselves from everything that contaminates body and spirit, perfecting holiness out of reverence for God (2 Corinthians 6:16b–7:1).

A ll potential requires conditions conducive to the maximum fulfillment of purpose. Consequently, all life forms have ideal conditions in which they grow and flourish. The apostle Paul clearly understood that the conditions in which we live affect the nature of our living. Righteousness that repeatedly associates with wickedness may, in time, be tarnished.

Paul's observations are as applicable today as they were when he wrote them. *"For what do righteousness and wickedness have in common? Or what fellowship can light have with darkness?"* (2 Cor. 6:14b). You cannot consistently spend time with ungodly people, or be surrounded by unrighteous behavior, and maintain your fellowship with God. Life outside your ideal environment will destroy your potential because a wrong environment always means death. *Fellowship with God and obedience to His laws and commandments are essential ingredients of your ideal environment.*

For we are God's workmanship, created in Christ Jesus to do good works, which God prepared in advance for us to do (Ephesians 2:10).

Dreams without work accomplish nothing. The apostle Paul could not have reached the non-Jewish world with the gospel of Jesus Christ if he had only rejoiced in his new relationship with God, learned to live by faith, surveyed his resources, and sought a healthy environment in which to live. Paul had to work to release his potential and to achieve his purpose.

The New Testament is filled with stories of Paul's efforts to share God's gift of salvation with those who had not heard the gospel. (See particularly Acts 13–20.) When one door closed, he looked for another. Again and again, Paul worked hard—fighting discouragement, misunderstandings, and distrust—to fulfill his commission from God.

Work releases potential and empowers success. It uses innate abilities and natural talents to share experience and proficiency. It also energizes the world's productive ability and activates man's creative power. *Work is the master key to releasing your potential.*

The Lord is exalted, for He dwells on high; He will fill Zion with justice and righteousness. He will be the sure foundation for your times, a rich store of salvation and wisdom and knowledge; the fear of the Lord is the key to this treasure (Isaiah 33:5-6).

Satan is our enemy. He wants to destroy the power of God within us so that God's glory is not revealed in us. Consequently, satan comes as a thief to steal our potential because he cannot boldly challenge God's power within us. The key to releasing God's power within you is reverencing Him, which is living with Him in a relationship of obedience and submission. *You are filled with heavenly wisdom, but you have to follow God's program to benefit from it.* Jesus spoke of this relationship with God in John 15:4-7.

Satan fears God's power within us because it is greater than he is. No wonder he tries to steal our potential. Therefore, our dreams, plans, and ideas are targets of his evil forces. The minute we have a good idea, the deceiver will send someone to criticize our dream because he cannot permit us to accomplish our vision. As long as we are only dreaming, he is safe and he'll let us alone.

Has he been lying to you about your dream?

Let us, therefore, make every effort to enter that rest, so that no one will fall by following their example of disobedience (Hebrews 4:11).

———————•—•———————

Satan's methods for stealing dreams are many and varied, according to the vision and the personality of the dreamer. Let us identify some of these *enemies of potential* so you will recognize them for what they are, the deceiver's activity in your life.

1. Disobedience.

The Bible repeatedly states that disobedience withholds God's blessings and rains His curses upon us. This is true because disobedience brings into our lives the natural (God-ordained) consequences of our actions. Teenagers who experiment with sex destroy the beauty of the first intimacy that God designed to be enjoyed between a husband and a wife, open themselves to AIDS and other diseases, and risk losing the joys of youth due to the birth of a child. They may also forfeit their dreams to problems in marriage in later years, to serious illnesses and possible death, and to the responsibilities of raising a child before they have matured into the task.

Disobedience always wastes potential and retards the attainment of goals. You cannot persist in disobedience and maximize your potential. To maximize your life you must submit to God's will in everything.

Blessed is the man whose sin the Lord will never count against him (Romans 4:8).

We are looking at the enemies of potential. The second enemy we face is:

2. Sin.

Although the effects of disobedience and sin are similar, sin is a more basic ill because it is total rebellion against the known will of God—or to say it another way, a declaration of independence from your Source. The resulting alienation from God destroys potential because we cannot know God if we do not have His Spirit, and His Spirit is the password to unlocking our potential. Sin says, "I know better than You do, God, how to run my life."

King David experienced the desolation and death that result from a rebellious spirit when he violated another man's wife and tried to cover up his action by having the woman's husband killed in battle and taking her for his wife. The son born to David from this affair died, and David endured the agony of separation from God. What the child could have done in his lifetime was sacrificed, as were David's energy and vitality during the months before he confessed his sin. Read David's prayer in Psalm 51:9-12.

Destroying your relationship with God through sin is always suicide.

To maximize your potential you must refuse to let sin get mastery over you.

For you did not receive a spirit that makes you a slave again to fear, but you received the Spirit of sonship. And by him we cry, "Abba, Father" (Romans 8:15).

We are continuing to look at the enemies of potential. The third enemy we face is:

3. Fear.

Fear is having faith in the impossible. It's dwelling on all that *could go wrong* instead of what *will go right*. Although, for example, accidents do happen and cars must be carefully maintained and driven, fear that prevents us from driving or riding in a car immobilizes our potential because it severely limits where we can go.

A spirit of self-discipline submits the information we receive through our bodies and our minds to the knowledge we receive from God's Spirit. It refuses to allow our minds to run wild imagining everything that *could* happen and chooses instead to apply God's promises to the situation and to depend on God. He who fears to try will never know what he could have done. He who fears God has nothing else to fear.

To maximize your life you must neutralize fear with faith.

Be strong and very courageous. Be careful to obey all the law my servant Moses gave you....Do not let this Book of the Law depart from your mouth; meditate on it day and night, so that you may be careful to do everything written in it. Then you will be prosperous and successful (Joshua 1:7-8).

The fourth enemy of potential that we face is:

4. Discouragement.

Most things worth having require patience and perseverance. No pianist plays perfectly the first time she touches the keys, nor does an athlete win a race the first time he runs. Many discouraging moments exist between an initial experience and the perfecting of a skill.

Unfortunately, *much potential is sacrificed on the altar of discouragement.* Replaying the music until it's right and running every day are the only ways to fulfill your potential. Concert pianists and Olympic athletes aren't born. They move beyond their discouraging moments to perfect their innate skills.

The same attitude is required of you to maximize your potential. *God will not give you a dream unless He knows you have the talents, abilities, and personality to complete it. His commands reveal the potential He gave you before you were born.*

To maximize your life you must neutralize discouragement with hope.

If you wait for perfect conditions, you will never get anything done (Ecclesiastes 11:4 TLB).

The fifth enemy of potential that we face is:

5. Procrastination.

How many times have you delayed so long in making a decision that it was made for you, or in completing a project that it was too late for your intended purpose? Most of us do this more often than we'd like to admit.

The Israelites discovered this when they found many reasons why they couldn't obey God and enter the land He was giving them. When they saw that the land was good, with an abundance of food, and finally decided to take the land as God had commanded them, they discovered that the opportunity to obey God was past. Disregarding God's warning that He would not go with them, they marched into battle and were soundly defeated.

When we become discouraged, we stop finding reasons for doing what we know we can do. Then God allows us to go our own way and suffer the consequences. Procrastination is a serious enemy of potential. It eats away at the very core of our time and motivation.

To maximize your life you must destroy procrastination by eliminating all excuses and reasons for not taking action. Just do it!

...I press on to take hold of that for which Christ Jesus took hold of me....Forgetting what is behind and straining toward what is ahead, I press on toward the goal to win the prize for which God has called me heavenward in Christ Jesus... (Philippians 3:12-16).

The sixth enemy of potential that we face is:

6. Past Failures.

Too often we are unwilling to take risks in the present because we have failed in the past. Perhaps the first story you sent to a magazine wasn't published, so you never wrote another story. Perhaps your first garden didn't produce many vegetables, so you never planted another garden. Perhaps your first business proposal didn't win the bank's approval, so you never started your own business, and you're still working for someone else.

The apostle Paul discovered the truth of this when he met Jesus. Paul had messed up, but in Christ he found the reason and the strength to pick himself up and move on. You must do the same or you will never see your full potential. Refuse to be a loser no matter how many times you lose. It is better to try and fail than never to try at all.

But Jesus would not entrust Himself to them, for He knew all men. He did not need man's testimony about man, for He knew what was in a man (John 2:24-25).

⸻◆⸻

The next enemy of potential that we face is:

7. The Opinions of Others.

Most of us have had the experience of sharing a great idea with friends only to have them tell us 50 reasons why it won't work. *Forsaking dreams because others belittle them or say we are crazy for trying them wastes potential.* Satan uses those closest to us, whose opinions we value, to get to our potential.

No human being can be trusted to defend your potential. You alone are responsible. By refusing to allow the disparaging comments of others to discourage you, by removing yourself from their influence when your vision becomes threatened, and by clinging to God's commandments and directions, you can unleash the totality of God's power within you.

Jesus demonstrated the importance of disregarding the opinions of others when He went to Jerusalem one Passover and the crowds believed in Him because of the miracles He performed. Yet Jesus would not entrust Himself to them, for *He knew all men.*

But Martha was distracted by all the preparations that had to be made. She came to Him and asked, "Lord, don't You care that my sister has left me to do the work by myself? Tell her to help me!" (Luke 10:40)

T he next enemy of potential that we face is:

8. Distractions.

This is one of the principal enemies of maximizing potential. All of us have had the experience of walking into another room and saying, "Now, why did I come here?"

Satan uses distractions to stop our progress toward a goal, or at least to change the speed of that progress. If he cannot convince us that our dream is wrong, he'll throw other things into our path to slow the development of our vision, or he'll push us and induce us to move ahead of God's timetable. One of satan's most successful devices is to preoccupy us with "good" things to distract us from the "right" things.

Because distractions take us off course, we cannot maximize our potential if we allow ourselves to be distracted from faithfully obeying Him every step of the way. Even though God, in His love and mercy, can get us back on course, we cannot recover the time and effort we wasted being distracted.

To maximize your potential keep yourself alert to distractions from the enemy.

I, even I, have spoken; yes, I have called him. I will bring him, and he will succeed in his mission (Isaiah 48:15).

The next enemy we face is:

9. Success.

Success is another enemy of potential. When we complete a task and quit because we think we've arrived, we never become all we are. If, for example, you graduate from college and teach first grade for the rest of your life when God wanted you to progress to becoming a principal, you forfeit much of your potential because you stopped at a preliminary success. *Leave your success and go create another. That's the only way you will release all your potential.*

Remember, satan is afraid of our potential. He knows that God created us to do something great. Therefore, he will allow us a small success and try to convince us that we have arrived.

In a similar manner, we must be careful to judge our successes by God's standards, not the world's. True success is being right with God and completing *His* assignment and purpose for our lives.

Follow Him as He leads you from success to success. To maximize your life you must never allow temporary achievement to cancel eternal fulfillment.

You have let go of the commands of God and are holding on to the traditions of men (Mark 7:8).

———•———

The next enemy of potential that we face is:

10. Tradition.

Traditions are powerful enemies of potential because they are full of security. We don't have to think when we do something the way we've always done it. Neither do we receive the incentive to grow and be creative because our new ideas may interfere with the conventional way of doing things.

The tragedy is that the tradition, which probably served its purpose well when it was started, may now prevent the accomplishment of the purpose for which it was established. *Use your imagination. Dream big and find new ways to respond to present situations and responsibilities.* Then you will uncover never-ending possibilities that inspire you to reach for continually higher achievements. We are sons of the "Creator," who created us to be creative. Nowhere in Scripture did God repeat an identical act.

Refrain from accepting or believing, "We've never done it that way before." Now is the time to try something different. To maximize your life you must be willing to release ineffective traditions for new methods.

Bad company corrupts good character
(1 Corinthians 15:33b).

We have been studying the enemies of potential. The next enemy we face is:

11. A Wrong Environment.

Nutritious vegetables cannot grow in poor soil and healthy fish cannot thrive in polluted waters. Neither can we maximize our potential in a wrong environment. The apostle Paul speaks to this principle when he says, *"Bad company corrupts good character."* That means, no matter how good our intentions may be, if we get in with bad company, we will eventually think and act as they do. We will not change them, they will change us.

Many dreams die because they are shared with the wrong people. Joseph learned that lesson the hard way. Indeed, he landed in a pit and was sold into slavery because his brothers were jealous of their father's favoritism toward him and they were offended by his dreams that placed him in authority over them. This is really not so surprising because older brothers rarely enjoy being dominated by younger ones. Had Joseph kept his dreams to himself, his brothers' resentment may not have developed into a plan to murder him.

Your greatest responsibility is to yourself, not others.

For what was glorious has no glory now in comparison with the surpassing glory. And if what was fading away came with glory, how much greater is the glory of that which lasts! (2 Corinthians 3:10-11)

The next two enemies we face are comparison and opposition:

12. Comparison.

Many parents struggle with the temptation to compare their children's strengths and weaknesses with the skills and temperaments of other children. This tendency to compare can be lethal to potential because it may produce either discouragement or false pride. Both prevent us from becoming all we can be. To maximize your life you must understand that you are unique, original, and irreplaceable. There is no comparison.

13. Opposition.

Satan has a way of snuffing out our great dreams by causing us to compromise. Most often this occurs because we give in to opposition. If he can't stop us, he'll push us to make a deal that is not God's deal. Opposition is natural to life and necessary for flight. If everyone agrees with your dream, it's probably a nightmare. To maximize your life you must accept and understand the nature and value of opposition.

We are hard pressed on every side, but not crushed; perplexed, but not in despair; persecuted, but not abandoned; struck down, but not destroyed (2 Corinthians 4:8-9).

The next enemy we face is:

14. Society's Pressure.

Pressure from society's standards and expectations is a threat to potential. The people we associate with, if they make judgments based on age, race, gender, financial status, ancestry, and education, may pressure us to relinquish a dream because they do not believe we can accomplish it.

Those who say "I can" no matter how many people say "you can't" transform dreams into realities. They have learned the priority of remaining true to their vision and they have developed the inner strength to trust God when society pushes them to abandon their goal.

You too must trust God and cooperate with Him to fulfill all the dreams He gives you and to reach all the goals He sets before you. Yes, satan will use the enemies of your potential to destroy God's power within you, but you are not captive to his ways.

Practicing the keys that maximize potential and recognizing the enemies of potential are essential steps in our journey of becoming who we are.

Be on your guard; stand firm in the faith;
be men of courage; be strong (1 Corinthians
16:13).

The boy sighed with satisfaction as the last of the four towers stood firm and tall. Now all he had to do to finish the sandcastle was to draw the design on the top of the walls. As he worked, he watched the approaching waves. The surf had been far down on the sand when he started building, but he knew the time would come when the waves would approach. He had built a large moat with an opening toward the sea to help the water stay in the moat instead of coming up over the entire castle.

The boy also kept an eye on his younger sister. Twice she had come to "help him." The first time she had smashed an entire section of the wall with her shovel. The last time he had been on guard and had seen her coming, thus protecting the castle from major destruction.

The boy building the sandcastle was wise. He recognized the approaching waves and the misguided help of his sister as enemies of his goal to build a castle and to play with his boats in its moat, and he defended against them.

Fight the good fight of the faith. Take hold of the eternal life to which you were called when you made your good confession in the presence of many witnesses (1 Timothy 6:12).

The defense of something occurs in two stages. Guarding is preventive in nature. It occurs while the *possibility* of an attack is present but before the threat is active and near. Guarding leads into the second step of defense, which is the action necessary when an enemy steps over the established boundary and threatens the treasure.

This second step of defense is *protecting*. *Protection* is active defense in the midst of an assault. Protecting and guarding work together. One without the other presents a weakened resistance to the thief who is trying to steal the treasure. The responsibility for this resistance lies with the recipient of the treasure. When God put Adam in the Garden, He didn't tell Heaven or the angels to protect the Garden. He told Adam to protect it.

This defense begins with an understanding of the treasure we have received from God and is worked out in our fight to keep what we have received. This treasure is both God's wisdom and power within us (our potential) and the gift of His Spirit.

"Now if you obey Me fully and keep My covenant, then out of all nations you will be My treasured possession..." (Exodus 19:5-6).

The defense of something occurs in two stages. *Guarding* is preventive in nature. *Protection* is active defense in the midst of an assault. It implements the pre-established plan to preserve the treasure from danger or harm.

As we have seen, God deposits a treasure in each person He creates. This treasure is (a) God's wisdom and knowledge concerning who He is, who we are, and how we are to live in relationship with Him; (b) God's power that worked in creation through the spoken word and even today brings forth beauty from chaos; and (c) God's Spirit who lives within our hearts.

Thus, God reveals Himself to us and crowns us with His potency—His power, authority, and strength to effectively accomplish what He wills.

But we have this treasure in jars of clay to show that this all-surpassing power is from God and not from us (2 Corinthians 4:7).

This potency of God within us—our potential—is the treasure we must defend. The treasure is the God-invested vision and purpose for our lives, designed both to show His glory and to bring Him glory.

The fear of the Lord is the beginning of knowledge, but fools despise wisdom and discipline (Proverbs 1:7).

The prophet Isaiah recognized God's wisdom as a treasure, as did the psalmists and King Solomon. They also agreed that the fear of the Lord is the key to this treasure:

He will be the sure foundation for your times, a rich store of salvation and wisdom and knowledge; the fear of the Lord is the key to this treasure (Isaiah 33:6).

The fear of the Lord is the beginning of wisdom; all who follow His precepts have good understanding... (Psalm 111:10). (See also Proverbs 2:1-6.)

What does it mean to fear God? The psalmists liken those who fear God with those who *"hope...in His unfailing love"* (Ps. 33:18), who *"understand [His] statutes"* (Ps. 119:79), and who *"walk in His ways"* (Ps. 128:1). They also compare fearing God with trusting Him (see Ps. 40:3; 115:11) and advise those who would learn what it means to fear the Lord to *"turn from evil and do good; seek peace and pursue it"* (see Ps. 34:11,14).

Thus, to fear the Lord is to trust and obey Him. In so doing we defend the deposit of His wisdom and knowledge within us.

Timothy, guard what has been entrusted to your care. Turn away from godless chatter and the opposing ideas of what is falsely called knowledge… (1 Timothy 6:20).

We don't think like God. Isaiah acknowledged this difference between God's thoughts and ours:

"For My thoughts are not your thoughts, neither are your ways My ways," declares the Lord. "As the heavens are higher than the earth, so are My ways higher than your ways and My thoughts than your thoughts. …so is My Word that goes out from My mouth: It will not return to Me empty, but will accomplish what I desire and achieve the purpose for which I sent it" (Isaiah 55:8-9,11).

This wisdom of God is a treasure to be cherished and defended. His thoughts toward us are good and His knowledge of us is perfect. He sees beyond our vessels of clay to His wisdom within us and calls forth from us what He sees. As we learn to see as God sees and to live from His perspective, we begin to understand this treasure of His wisdom and the importance of safeguarding it from the snares of the evil one. Paul wrote of this to Timothy.

God's wisdom will always surpass the ways of the world.

*And said: "O Lord, God of our fathers, are
You not the God who is in heaven? You rule
over all the kingdoms of the nations. Power
and might are in Your hand, and no one can
withstand You* (2 Chronicles 20:6).

God has also deposited His power within us. The
apostle Paul spoke of this power as the means
by which God works salvation in us—*"I am not
ashamed of the gospel, because it is the power of
God for the salvation of everyone who believes..."*
(Rom. 1:16)—and he carefully portrayed this salvation as *"...a demonstration of the Spirit's power, so
that* [our] *faith might not rest on men's wisdom, but
on God's power"* (1 Cor. 2:4-5).

In a similar manner, Peter and John understood
God's power to be the secret behind their power:

*"...Men of Israel, why does this surprise
you? Why do you stare at us as if by our
own power or godliness we had made this
man walk?...By faith in the name of Jesus,
this man whom you see and know was made
strong..."* (Acts 3:12,16a).

God doesn't want us just to *know* who we are in
Him; He wants us to *become* it.

But thanks be to God, who always leads us in triumphal procession in Christ and through us spreads everywhere the fragrance of the knowledge of Him (2 Corinthians 2:14).

P aul identifies the Holy Spirit Himself as the deposit or treasure within us that we must guard and protect.

Now it is God who makes both us and you stand firm in Christ. He anointed us, set His seal of ownership on us, and put His Spirit in our hearts as a deposit, guaranteeing what is to come (2 Corinthians 1:21-22).

Now it is God who has made us...and has given us the Spirit as a deposit, guaranteeing what is to come (2 Corinthians 5:5).

The Holy Spirit both reveals God's wisdom and power in us and guarantees that we will receive all God has planned for those who seek His wisdom and live by His power. His presence in our lives is an important deposit because He is the key to tapping into God's storehouse of wisdom and power.

Through Him we know God's thoughts and understand what God has given to us:

We have not received the spirit of the world but the Spirit who is from God, that we may understand what God has freely given us (1 Corinthians 2:12).

Guard the good deposit that was entrusted to you—guard it with the help of the Holy Spirit who lives in us (2 Timothy 1:14).

In essence, God's wisdom, power, and Spirit are the treasure we must safeguard. They are a deposit of Himself in us so that we can act and function like Him, sharing in His work. Together they are our potential, the source of our dreams and visions. We must remember, however, that having this deposit of God does not mean that we will keep it.

All the great things God has put inside us—our visions, dreams, plans, and talents—are satan's targets. He is afraid of men and women who have faith in God's wisdom and power, because they take their visions and translate them into action.

The deceiver fears the treasure we possess. His attack is so severe that Paul advised Timothy to seek the help of the Holy Spirit to meet and overcome it. God has given us everything we need to safeguard our hidden wealth from the schemes and deceit of the evil one. The Holy Spirit, sent by Jesus when we receive Him as Savior, is our Helper.

Therefore put on the full armor of God, so that when the day of evil comes, you may be able to stand your ground, and after you have done everything, to stand (Ephesians 6:13).

———————— ◆ ————————

The description of the armor of God in Ephesians chapter 6 details a plan to guard and protect your life against satan's invasion. You must understand the provisions of this plan and put them into practice if you want to defend your potential.

First, recognize your enemy as the spiritual forces of evil, *"For our struggle is not against flesh and blood, but against...the powers of this dark world and against the spiritual forces of evil..."* (Eph. 6:12). What looks to be a conflict in personalities or a difference in values may well be a struggle on a more basic level. Discouragement, opposition, criticism, and the other enemies of potential are the work of evil forces through those who are close to you. Learn to recognize and combat these obstacles for what they are.

Although death is a favorite way for satan to destroy potential, he will most likely try to ensnare you with one of the enemies of potential. Be alert to recognize these enemies for what they are—satan's attacks on your potential.

For our struggle is not against flesh and blood, but against the rulers, against the authorities, against the powers of this dark world and against the spiritual forces of evil in the heavenly realms (Ephesians 6:12).

No matter what you do, you will always have critics. This is true because some people cannot bear to see others succeed. When you aren't doing anything, you're not a problem for them; but when you start fulfilling your dreams and visions, you'll attract attention. People don't care about you until you start doing something big.

Learn to expect their opposition and to rise above it. Refuse to get drawn into their petty quarrels or to allow their words and actions to influence your self-esteem or your behavior. *Every dream you share has the potential to cause jealousy*, so be careful with whom you share your dreams.

Others who are pursuing their purpose and maximizing their potential will understand your behavior, even if they can't see your particular vision. Find them and enjoy their company—those who are going somewhere are more likely to support you in your journey. This is an essential factor in guarding your potential.

Put on the full armor of God so that you can take your stand against the devil's schemes (Ephesians 6:11).

———•———

We need to learn how to defend our potential. *One way you can prepare to defend your potential is to* **make wise choices**. Consider carefully with whom you associate and where you spend your time. Be cautious with whom you share your dreams—if you share them at all.

A second priority in preparing to meet satan's attack is to **be sure that your vision is from God.** Don't conjure up your own ideas. If they contradict God's Word, you know your ideas are not from Him. God will not deny His Word. False dreams and fake prophecies are sure ways to lose your potential. Satan will distract you any way he can. Prepare for his attack by staying in close fellowship with God and by seeking His knowledge and wisdom.

A third method for fortifying yourself against the assault of evil is to **seek God's discipline and direction in your life.** Be truthful in your dealings. Act with justice and virtue. Live at peace with others in so far as it is within your power, being careful, however, not to compromise your loyalty and obedience to God and His Word.

Stand firm then, with the belt of truth buckled around your waist...Take the helmet of salvation and the sword of the Spirit, which is the Word of God (Ephesians 6:14,17).

———◆———

When Nehemiah was seeking to rebuild the wall that protected Jerusalem he faced opposition. Over time Nehemiah's enemies became increasingly hostile. (See Nehemiah 4:11-15.)

If you are accomplishing something, at first you may have a critic who is annoyed by you, but if you persist in your work, he or she may become incensed.

Protect your potential from attack by *allowing God to fight for you* (see Neh. 4:20). *Don't allow a lull in the battle to convince you that the war is over. Don't confuse quiet with peace.*

When Nehemiah's enemies received word that the wall had been completely rebuilt, they requested a meeting. Nehemiah wisely countered, recognizing it as a different kind of attack (see Neh. 6:2b-3).

You too must *remain firm in your decisions and refuse to be intimidated by your oppressors. Stay away from the opposition. Don't waste time talking.*

Nehemiah used many methods to fight for his vision. You must employ the same methods to preserve your potential from attack.

Folly delights a man who lacks judgment, but a man of understanding keeps a straight course (Proverbs 15:21).

There will always be people who are committed to destroying you. They will criticize you, ridicule you, and become angry with you. Ignore them. You are not responsible for their actions, only your own.

Fight for your vision. Share your dream only when you must, and choose carefully with whom you share it. Expect opposition and be careful not to allow the threats and accusations of your enemies to intimidate you. Stick with your decisions and remain committed to your goal. Talk to God about your needs and allow Him to respond to your oppressors. Never answer them yourself.

Finally, keep yourself busy. *Don't allow the battle to interfere with your work*. You may not be popular, but you will be successful because God works with those who put forth the effort to stay with the vision He has given them. Thus, *your opposers will learn that they are not as important as what you are doing*, and you will remain focused on your vision with renewed wisdom and strength to accomplish it. Your potential is worth the effort of overcoming its enemies.

We work hard with our own hands. When we are cursed, we bless; when we are persecuted, we endure it (1 Corinthians 4:12).

God helps those who help themselves. This familiar saying expresses an important truth. Paul told Timothy to seek the help of the Holy Spirit (see 2 Tim. 1:14), not to expect Him to run the whole show. The Holy Spirit will not take over our lives, but He will assist *us* in running them. He is our helper or assistant. He doesn't guard our potential. He helps us to do so by guiding our decisions and by empowering us to withstand and triumph in the midst of trials.

God won't take a bad habit or an inappropriate lifestyle from you because He didn't give it to you. He *will* affirm your decisions and strengthen your efforts when you start taking positive steps to *rid yourself* of the negative influences, the wrong attitudes, or the poor choices that are threatening your potential. If you stay stuck in your present rut with no attempts to get out of it, your dreams will wither and die. You must work together to protect your potential.

The future of your dreams and visions is at stake.

But grow in the grace and knowledge of our Lord and Savior Jesus Christ. To Him be glory both now and forever! Amen (2 Peter 3:18).

The old woman smiled as she entered the small, hot room. A blaze of color met her eyes. African violets of many colors bloomed. After the last of her children had left home, she had become very depressed and had little to do. That's when a friend had given her clippings from her African violets and had persuaded her to turn the playroom into a greenhouse. The idea had been a good one, giving her renewed interest in life.

Even the day her husband had died, she had wandered in here to find solace among her friends—as she had come to think of her plants.

After nearly 40 years of hard work and extensive reading, the riotous color that surrounded her revealed the success of her efforts. Now, her skill in cultivating and breeding African violets was known throughout the community, and over the years she had found great joy in teaching others the art of cultivating plants.

The successful fulfillment of your potential is similar to the task of growing prizewinning flowers. Both require careful attention and diligent effort to produce winning results.

He has lost connection with the Head, from whom the whole body, supported and held together by its ligaments and sinews, grows as God causes it to grow (Colossians 2:19).

You may have the potential to be a world-class architect, but your ability does not guarantee that you will reach this level of success. You may never progress beyond drawing doll house plans for your daughter or designing a model train layout for your son.

An important key is spending the necessary time and effort to promote the development of your talent. *You must cultivate and feed your potential.*

God created all life to depend on cultivation to maximize its existence because potential cannot be released without work. In essence, God said, "I can't allow these trees and plants to grow yet because they need cultivation when they start growing and there is no one to care for them."

The New International Version of the Bible says that God gave Adam the responsibility of *working* the Garden. The Revised Standard Version and the King James Version describe man's task as that of *tilling* the Garden, and the Good News Bible speaks of *cultivating*. All point to man's assignment to help the Garden produce to its fullest capacity.

You were running a good race. Who cut in on you and kept you from obeying the truth? (Galatians 5:7)

Potential is like soil. It must be worked and fed to produce fruit. King Solomon referred to this process of releasing the fruitfulness of man when he said, *"The purposes of a man's heart are deep waters, but a man of understanding draws them out"* (Prov. 20:5). Notice, the drawing out of man's potential requires effort.

The apostle Paul understood this need to put forth the effort to release his fruitfulness:

> *Do you not know that in a race all the runners run, but only one gets the prize? Run in such a way as to get the prize.... Therefore I do not run like a man running aimlessly; I do not fight like a man beating the air. No, I beat my body and make it my slave so that after I have preached to others, I myself will not be disqualified for the prize* (1 Corinthians 9:24,26-27).

The primary principle in cultivating one's life for maximum living is to destroy ignorance by the pursuit of knowledge, wisdom, and understanding.

By wisdom a house is built, and through understanding it is established (Proverbs 24:3).

————•————

Maximizing our potential requires a process. Think of it this way. Suppose I wanted to create a beautiful vase to place in my living room, but I knew nothing about making pottery. My first step would need to be a visit to a master potter, or at least to the local library, to learn all I could about working clay into beautiful pieces. I would have to learn about the selection and preparation of the clay, etc. Much work, including many hours of practice on much lesser pots than the vase I hoped to create, would precede my reaching the goal of making a vase to place in my living room.

This procedure is not unlike the process we must undertake to maximize our potential. Knowledge and effort must coexist, but knowledge is the foundation for success. As we saw in the last chapter, God's wisdom and knowledge become available to us when we are connected to Him through the presence of His Spirit. An understanding of His ways and the discovery of His purposes are part of the treasure He has given us.

Apply your heart to instruction and your ears to words of knowledge (Proverbs 23:12).

The search for knowledge requires effort. You must seek it like a treasure that is precious to you. You cannot touch God's knowledge, however, without diligence and exertion.

My son, if you accept my words and store up my commands within you, turning your ear to wisdom and applying your heart to understanding, and if you call out for insight and cry aloud for understanding, and if you look for it as for silver and search for it as for hidden treasure, then you will understand the fear of the Lord and find the knowledge of God (Proverbs 2:1-5).

By wisdom a house is built, and through understanding it is established; through knowledge its rooms are filled with rare and beautiful treasures. A wise man has great power, and a man of knowledge increases strength; for waging war you need guidance, and for victory many advisers (Proverbs 24:3-6).

Knowledge must always precede action or much time and effort will be wasted through misguided efforts and dead-end directions. God, who planned your life and granted you the potential to fulfill His plans, works for and with you when you seek to know Him and to understand and follow His ways.

Wise men store up knowledge, but the mouth of a fool invites ruin (Proverbs 10:14).

Sadly, we often forfeit our potential because we neglect the wisdom, knowledge, and understanding that come from God alone. Solomon spoke of the consequences of this neglect, as did the prophet Hosea (see Prov. 13:14-16; Hos. 4:6).

A lack of knowledge is not the same as the unavailability of knowledge. Hosea says that God's people perish because they have *rejected* knowledge. Knowledge may surround us, but unless we apply it to our situation or use it to inform our decisions, it is useless to us. We cannot really excuse ourselves before the Lord saying, "I didn't know," because opportunities to gain knowledge abound in our world. We live in an age of an information explosion with libraries, tape ministries, teaching videos, television, and radio bombarding us on every side with opportunities to stretch our horizons and increase our knowledge.

No matter how great your dream is, you must have the information relative to your plan.

"My people are destroyed from lack of knowledge. Because you have rejected knowledge, I also reject you as My priests; because you have ignored the law of your God, I also will ignore your children" (Hosea 4:6).

The devil doesn't destroy God's people...the government doesn't destroy God's people...the economy doesn't destroy God's people...cocaine and marijuana don't destroy God's people. *Ignorance* destroys God's people. This one thing is behind every destructive influence in our lives.

God rejects those who reject His knowledge. Ignorance affects how God answers our prayers because we ask for things we don't need or shouldn't want. To ask rightly we must understand how we operate, how the devil operates, how the world operates, and how God operates.

God also ignores the children of those who ignore His knowledge. This is true because your children learn what you know. If you don't know anything, they aren't going to learn anything, and they will thus make the same mistakes and have the same values and attitudes you have.

Ignorance messes up the next generation. Our world is experiencing a multitude of human disasters that give evidence to this fact. Abortion, AIDS, environmental issues, drugs—all reveal the consequences of the rejection of knowledge by this generation and those that preceded us.

The teaching of the wise is a fountain of life, turning a man from the snares of death. Good understanding wins favor, but the way of the unfaithful is hard. Every prudent man acts out of knowledge, but a fool exposes his folly (Proverbs 13:14-16).

So many of us ignore the knowledge of God and His will. *Our ignorance of God's will and His ways has twisted our world. We devalue what God values and elevate what is insignificant to Him.* He sees the tremendous ability we have and we look at the earth houses that contain that treasure (see 2 Cor. 4:7).

Our poverty of knowledge is revealed by our inability to fulfill God's potential on our own. We live aimlessly without purpose, flitting from one thing to another and never accomplishing anything. Such life is a waste of time. Without a sense of purpose we are like stillborn babies.

Your potential will be wasted if you do not allow God to cleanse your sight and redirect your values. Then you can escape this purposeless existence. This occurs as you become aware of the world's standards and compare them carefully with God's. You may be surprised by what you find.

*Jesus said, "My kingdom is not of this world.
If it were, My servants would fight to prevent
My arrest by the Jews. But now My kingdom
is from another place"* (John 18:36).

The Bible says, "...*Man looks at the outward appearance, but the Lord looks at the heart*" (1 Sam. 16:7). It's time you and I reevaluate the standards of the world. Our cars are faster but weaker. Our clothes are sharper, but they come apart at the seams. Our vinyl shoes shine nicely, but they lack the durability of leather. What appears to be better may indeed be a compromise on value and worth. These upside-down values are attacking your potential.

Our world is sick because we value the wrong things.

The values and standards of our world are not so different from those of the Pharisees. We save whales and try to protect endangered species, but we allow babies to be aborted. We cannot shoot flamingos, but we can take a scalpel and kill human fetuses.

The most damaging pollutants that are poisoning our communities are not coming from cars, factories, and toxic waste dumps. They come from bookshelves, televisions, movie houses, and rental videos.

He is like a tree planted by streams of water, which yields its fruit in season and whose leaf does not wither. Whatever he does prospers (Psalm 1:3).

Potential must be cultivated and fed to produce fruit. But how do we do this? How do we cultivate and feed the talents, skills, and abilities we possess?

The definitions of *cultivate* imply that the process is to be beneficial, not harmful. If the provisions do not supply nourishment that is essential for growth, they are not truly feeding us. Likewise, if the activity and attention do not help us to develop, refine, improve, and promote our abilities, skills, and talents, they cannot truly be called cultivation.

Even as seeds do not become plants overnight, so the wealth of our potential cannot be exposed and fulfilled in an instant. As specific plants require certain nutrients and conditions to grow, so we must provide the right nourishment and environment to encourage the maximizing of our potential. These specifications have been set by God, who created us. To ignore them is to invite death. We must exert effort to cultivate what God has given us, and we must exercise care to fertilize and water it properly.

*Consecrate yourselves and be holy, because
I am the Lord your God* (Leviticus 20:7).

We are like a fallow field. If we activate and stimulate our potential through challenging work and experiences, but we neglect to provide the appropriate fertilizers that will sustain and maintain it within those situations, before long growth will become stunted and eventually stop. Likewise, if we feed our bodies, souls, and spirits according to our Manufacturer's specifications, but we fail to foster and develop occasions when we can try new things and reach for new goals, we will still diminish the effective release of our potential. Both cultivating and feeding are necessary for wholesome growth.

Each dimension of our potential—body, soul, and spirit—has definite specifications and materials for cultivation and explicit requirements in fertilizers. You are what you eat. This is true for all three dimensions of potential. If you eat excessive fatty foods, you will gain weight and your face will be covered with pimples. If you feed your mind with trash, your thoughts will be in the gutter. If you feed your spirit the information received through the senses of your body and the education of your soul, neglecting God's wisdom and knowledge, you will operate from worldly standards and values.

...offer your bodies as living sacrifices, holy and pleasing to God—this is your spiritual act of worship (Romans 12:1).

Your body is a precise machine that requires proper food, exercise, and rest. Healthy food, regular exercise, and scheduled periods of rest are essential for it to operate at its maximum potential. Physical health deteriorates when sweets, fats, or other harmful foods are stuffed into the body, and the body's strength and endurance are lessened if exercise (work) is missing from your daily routine.

The cultivation and feeding of your body requires that you use it with discretion, setting it apart for its intended uses. Consider the proper use of your body when you are working or exercising. For example, safeguard your back by bending your knees to lift a heavy load.

You must cultivate your physical body by preserving it and protecting it from pollutants. If you are going to do something for the world, if you are really going to contribute to the effectiveness and the productivity of your nation, you cannot be sick because you cannot be effective if you are sick.

You are responsible to protect your physical temple. Cultivate your body.

Finally, brothers, whatever is true, whatever is noble, whatever is right, whatever is pure, whatever is lovely, whatever is admirable...think about such things (Philippians 4:8).

It's a pity to die with water when people are dying of thirst. Yet it happens every day as people who have the answers to the world's problems refuse to feed and cultivate their minds so they can reach into the deep wells of their possibilities and pull out what the world needs. Look to the careful cultivation and feeding of your mind. Remember, the person who *doesn't* read is no better off than the person who *can't* read.

The cultivation of your soul also includes the discipline of your will. Discipline is training or teaching someone or something to obey a particular command or to live by a certain standard. The discipline of your will is particularly important because the will is the decision maker. If you refuse to discipline your will, you won't be successful in fulfilling your potential because your will determines your decisions, which govern your potential.

The cultivating of your soul also requires that you control your emotions. Too often we allow our emotions to control us instead of our controlling them.

Jesus answered, "It is written: 'Man does not live on bread alone'" (Luke 4:4).

Maximizing your potential begins with your decision to accept Jesus Christ as your Lord and Savior because the measure of your true potential is your spirit. Until you become reconnected with God through faith in Jesus Christ and the presence of His Spirit in your heart, you are spiritually dead, and the potential of your spirit is unavailable to you.

Those who live according to the sinful nature have their minds set on what that nature desires; but those who live in accordance with the Spirit have their minds set on what the Spirit desires. The mind of sinful man is death, but the mind controlled by the Spirit is life and peace (Romans 8:5-6).

The secret wisdom of God concerning your potential (see 1 Cor. 2:7-11) cannot influence your life if His Spirit is not present in your heart because only God's Spirit knows and understands God's plans and purposes for you. These were written long before your birth. Attaining your maximum potential becomes possible when you cultivate and feed your spirit by hooking yourself up to God and abiding in Him. (See John 15:1-8.)

Command them to do good, to be rich in good deeds, and to be generous and willing to share (1 Timothy 6:18).

———❖———

Silently the orchestra waited. What would this new masterpiece of their beloved conductor be like? He had promised that it would be different from anything he had ever written.

When they started to play, it soon became evident that no one had the lead. The longer they played, the stranger the music became.

The maestro passed out another set of music. When he lifted his baton, anticipation filled each face. This time beautiful music filled the room.

After the orchestra had played for a few minutes, the conductor stopped them and asked, "Do you understand what I have done? If you look at the notes on the two scores, you will notice that they are the same. But the rests are different. On the second score they were considerably fewer and were at fitting places. The first time, you never played together. I did this to show you that each part is important, but meaningless without the others. When we all play the right notes at the right time, blending the music and sharing the unique sounds of each instrument, a beautiful melody emerges."

In a large house there are articles not only of gold and silver, but also of wood and clay; some are for noble purposes and some for ignoble....useful to the Master and prepared to do any good work (2 Timothy 2:20-21).

Everything God called into being He gave a purpose that meshes with the larger purpose of the world. He doesn't need our involvement to accomplish all He is capable of doing and being, but He wants us to enjoy the blessing of participating in His purpose. *Your gifts, talents, and abilities are your share of the endowment God gives to mankind to bless all creation.*

God finds satisfaction in watching you discover and use your potential. Thus, God gets excited when you take authority over your bad habits. Sometimes it would be easier for God to just snap His fingers and take over, but then He'd lose the joy of watching you order your life and the pleasure of seeing you expose His potential.

God has shared His potential with you, now He wants to enjoy the benefits of that gift. His joy overflows when you release all He has given you.

Therefore, as we have opportunity, let us do good to all people, especially to those who belong to the family of believers (Galatians 6:10).

When I was in college, I went on a tour of Europe. After several days, I lost interest in all I was seeing because my fiancée, who is now my wife, was not there to share it with me. On that trip I learned the truth of this principle: *Potential is never given for itself. Whatever God gives to you, He gives for others.*

To be solitary or alone is not the same as being single. To be alone is to be isolated and cut off from others. Communication is impossible because you have no one like yourself to share with. This is what God says is not good.

To be single is to be unmarried. Marriage is not a requirement or a prerequisite for the fulfillment of your potential. You do not necessarily *need* a husband or a wife. What you do need, however, is someone with whom you can share your potential.

Do not envy wicked men, do not desire their company (Proverbs 24:1).

Neither two males nor two females can produce a baby because man's potential is fulfilled by sharing it with a woman, and woman's is fulfilled by sharing it with a man. For their potential to be fruitful, men and women must share their physical potential within the context of a male-female relationship that is within the bonds of marriage.

What is known today as an "alternative lifestyle" is truly the abuse of natural destiny and the violation of human nature because it prevents this fulfillment of purpose. Woman was created to receive, and man was created to give. Thus, their shared potentials complement each other. Two givers or two receivers cannot work together to produce fruit. Be careful that you share your physical potential with the right person.

The potential of your soul is fulfilled by sharing it within the context of the family. Here a child learns to give and receive love and affection. Very often psychological and emotional problems arise when love is not felt and expressed in the formative years.

Give to him as the Lord your God has blessed you (Deuteronomy 15:14b).

———————

*P*otential is fulfilled only when it is given to others. You cannot enjoy or fulfill your potential if you keep it to yourself.* Everything God gave you, He gave for me and everyone else. He blesses you with additional gifts when you use the blessings you have already received to bless others. This is true because sharing your potential both reveals hidden possibilities and releases additional gifts. If anything along the way chooses to withhold its potential—be it the seed, the tree, or the fruit—the cycle is broken and much potential is lost.

This same truth is evident in the music of an orchestra. The instruments' potential to produce music cannot be fulfilled until the individual notes are released by the players. If even one player refuses to release what he possesses, the loss extends far beyond the one who withholds his contribution because the withheld potential of one affects the potential of all. All suffer loss—musicians and music—if even one person or one instrument refuses to cooperate. Only as all give of what they possess can the potential of the music be released.

In everything I did, I showed you that by this kind of hard work we must help the weak, remembering the words the Lord Jesus Himself said: "It is more blessed to give than to receive" (Acts 20:35).

Treasures that are hidden and locked up benefit no one. Say, for example, that your grandmother gave you a beautiful necklace that she wore as a bride. If you keep it locked in a safe and never wear it, its beauty is wasted.

Or perhaps you have wedding gifts of beautiful china, sterling silver, and fine crystal that you have never used to serve a meal. You're wasting the potential of those dishes. They cannot do what they are supposed to do sitting in a box. People bought them for you to use. *Treasure is useless unless you expose it.* Potential can never be attained if it has no opportunity to give.

This was the power of John F. Kennedy's words, spoken at his inauguration to be the president of the United States: "Ask not what your country can do for you, but what you can do for your country." Kennedy's words prompt us to focus on what we can give instead of what we can get.

How great is the love the Father has lavished on us, that we should be called children of God! And that is what we are! The reason the world does not know us is that it did not know Him (1 John 3:1).

God is constantly releasing seeds into the soil of your life. He is a Giver and He created you to be like Him. The foundation of God's giving nature is revealed in His purpose for creating men and women.

God made Adam and Eve so He would have someone to love and bless—more children like Christ, His Incarnate Son. Although God possessed all He had created, those things were useless to Him until He created humankind to release their potential by using His creations and, thereby, showing off His fullness.

You are the object of God's love. Because love can be fulfilled only when the receiver of love is like the giver, He created you like Himself, to be loved by Him and to love as He loves.

They are always generous and lend freely;
their children will be blessed (Psalm 37:26).

Think about the last time you bought a card or a gift for a spouse or a close friend. Much of the pleasure in giving the gift is found in choosing something that will delight the one to whom you are giving it. The gift's meaning is found in the shared love of the giver and the recipient.

This is the meaning of Jesus' words: *"Do not give dogs what is sacred; do not throw your pearls to pigs. If you do, they may trample them under their feet, and then turn and tear you to pieces"* (Matt. 7:6).

A pet cannot appreciate a diamond ring, but your sweetheart will. Why? She understands the thoughts and the feelings that both prompted the gift and are revealed in it. The one who receives a gift must understand and appreciate the giver before the gift can have meaning. Love is released through giving.

Jesus Christ gave the seed that brings new life by releasing His potential to be a Savior.

The fruit of the righteous is a tree of life, and he who wins souls is wise (Proverbs 11:30).

———◆———

Blessings are never given solely for the benefit of the one who receives them. That means all God has given you—your clothes, food, house, car, bike, education, intelligence, personality, etc.—are given to you so you can maximize them by sharing them. You cannot release the full potential of anything if you do not share it.

God operates from this perspective: "I'm going to share with you so you will be blessed by My sharing and you, in turn, will bless others by your sharing." He gives to you so you can share His potential by being motivated to pass on all He gives you.

God finds joy in giving to you so you can give to others. He blesses you to bless another. No matter what your circumstances are, there is some way you can share your potential with others. If you are homebound, give yourself through prayer or the ministry of encouragement through cards, letters, and phone calls. Or perhaps you are retired with few financial resources but much time. Pour yourself into a child.

Your gifts are for me and my gifts are for you. Together we can bless the world.

Look at the birds of the air; they do not sow or reap or store away in barns, and yet your heavenly Father feeds them. Are you not much more valuable than they? (Matthew 6:26)

---

*T*rue joy is found not in what you accomplish but in who benefits from your success. Dying to yourself and giving for me and others will reap for you the joy of seeing your efforts reproduced many times over in us. Your sharing will give life to many.

If, however, you refuse to share, you will destroy both God's joy in giving to you and your joy in passing on what He gives. You will also forfeit His blessings because those who wish to receive from the abundance of God must use all He gives wisely. This is true because selfishness concerns itself only with its own prosperity and well-being. It lacks interest in the concerns and needs of others.

You cannot emulate the giving nature of God if you retain all you have for your own wants and needs; neither can your bucket draw from the deep waters in me or in others. Such selfishness kills potential and lessens the likelihood that you will be blessed by our potential.

*Now all has been heard...for God will
bring every deed into judgment, including
every hidden thing, whether it is good or
evil* (Ecclesiastes 12:13-14).

———◆———

Y ou were created to give. When you lavish your
potential on yourself, your potential and all you
accomplish by using it lose their meaning. King
Solomon learned this when he went through life
doing one thing after another for himself.

*"Meaningless! Meaningless!" says the
Teacher. "Utterly meaningless! Everything
is meaningless." What does man gain from
all his labor at which he toils under the sun?
...I undertook great projects...I made gardens and parks and planted all kinds of
fruit trees in them. I made reservoirs...I
refused my heart no pleasure. My heart
took delight in all my work, and this was
the reward for all my labor. Yet when I surveyed all that my hands had done and what
I had toiled to achieve, everything was
meaningless...*

*So I hated life, because the work that is
done under the sun was grievous to me. All
of it is meaningless, a chasing after the
wind* (Ecclesiastes 1:2-3; 2:4-6,10-11,17).

Work and effort that focus on self are meaningless. It doesn't matter what you accomplish, none of
it will bring you satisfaction unless you give from
what you have.

By Myself I can do nothing; I judge only as I hear, and My judgment is just, for I seek not to please Myself but Him who sent Me (John 5:30).

Near the end of His life, Jesus reminded His disciples that they could not accomplish anything apart from Him. The same is true for our lives. Without this consistent association with God, our fruitfulness suffers and we become no more than a branch to be thrown into the fire. The power of potential is gone. (See John 15.)

This absence of power hurts both the person who has withdrawn from God and God Himself. He created us to bear fruit that reflects His nature and glory. When we neglect to fulfill this purpose, we grieve the heart of God.

God's pleasure in Jesus was evident when He spoke from a cloud at the time of Jesus' baptism and again on the mountain of transfiguration (see Matt. 3:17; 17:5). The source of His pleasure was Jesus' willingness to fulfill the purpose for which He had been sent into the world and to release His potential (see John 8:29; 17:4-6,10,13).

This is how we know what love is: Jesus Christ laid down His life for us. And we ought to lay down our lives for our brothers (1 John 3:16).

In all my prayers for all of you, I always pray with joy because of your partnership in the gospel from the first day until now, being confident of this, that He who began a good work in you will carry it on to completion until the day of Christ Jesus (Philippians 1:4-6).

Partnership speaks of sharing. When we fail to share our potential, this partnership is forfeited and the fruit for which we were chosen and appointed is lost.

God mourns for this loss because the loss of potential limits His activity on earth and destroys the joy of sharing—for God, for ourselves, and for those with whom we might have shared. Selfishness always destroys the joy of giving.

Your selfishness in keeping the treasure to yourself ultimately destroys the very gift that is the source of your wealth. *Potential that is not shared self-destructs.*

You did not choose Me, but I chose you and appointed you to go and bear fruit—fruit that will last. Then the Father will give you whatever you ask in My name (John 15:16).

For where you have envy and selfish ambition, there you find disorder and every evil practice (James 3:16).

S*elfishness destroys the cycle of giving initiated by God.* Very often you have not because you lavish upon yourself all you have received. God will give you all things if you ask to receive so you may pass them on to others. I'm blessed because I have a passion to pass on to you all that God has given to me.

Give, and it will be given to you. A good measure, pressed down, shaken together and running over, will be poured into your lap. For with the measure you use, it will be measured to you (Luke 6:38).

Some of you are blessed with tremendous talents, gifts, and knowledge. I wonder what is happening to them. Flow with your God-given abilities. Use them to bless others and to glorify God. Don't worry if your gifts and talents aren't as grand as you'd like. Use them to benefit others, and you will see them grow. *Sharing all God has given you is a must if you want to maximize your potential.*

*One generation will commend Your works
to another; they will tell of Your mighty acts*
(Psalm 145:4).

History is made by individuals who dare to challenge and exceed the accepted norm. Why follow a path when you can make a trail? It is incumbent upon each of us to ask ourselves the following questions: Have we become all we are capable of? Have we extended ourselves to the maximum? Have we done the best we can do? Have we used our gifts, talents, and abilities to their limit?

Everything is designed by God not only to reproduce itself but also to transfer its life and treasure to the next generation. Potential is not fully maximized until it reproduces itself in the following generation.

An old Chinese proverb that states, *"The end of a thing is greater than its beginning,"* rings true for our lives. King Solomon concurred with this truth: *"...The race is not to the swift or the battle to the strong..."* (Eccles. 9:11). Every individual is therefore responsible to live to the fullest for the sake of the following generation.

Now he who supplies seed to the sower and bread for food will also supply and increase your store of seed and will enlarge the harvest of your righteousness (2 Corinthians 9:10).

I will never forget the day I first discovered seedless fruit. One of the pleasures I enjoy within my very busy schedule is accompanying my wife to the food store, which gives us time to plan our family meals and discover new items together.

On one of these occasions, I was intrigued to see a large sign introducing seedless grapes and oranges. I rejoiced at the prospect of being able to enjoy grapes for the first time without the inconvenience of having to eject the seeds. I picked up two pounds of red and white grapes and a bag of oranges, looking forward to eating them at home.

In the midst of my eating pleasure, I realized that, "If these grapes and oranges have no seeds, how can they reproduce another generation of fruit?" The fruit was beautiful, ripe, sweet, juicy, and pleasing to eat, but it lacked the potential to transfer its uniqueness to another generation. *In reality the tree is not in the fruit but in the seed.*

For as the soil makes the sprout come up and a garden causes seeds to grow, so the Sovereign Lord will make righteousness and praise spring up before all nations (Isaiah 61:11).

Please note that the seed in yesterday's example did fulfill part of its purpose. It germinated, grew, developed, and even bore fruit. Yet the totality of its potential was not fulfilled because it did not extend itself to the maximum potential of releasing seeds. Because the seed failed to reproduce itself, the next generation of trees was robbed of life, consequently affecting the entire human race and all creation. This is the impact when one element in nature withholds its true potential and refuses to maximize itself.

Tragically, there are millions of people who exist in "seedless lives." They are conceived, grow, and develop; they dress up, smell good, and look good; and they even pretend to be happy. Yet they have no sense of generational responsibility. They have no idea of their duty to the future. No man is born to live or die to himself. When a seed maximizes its potential, it not only feeds the next generation but also guarantees its continuance through the seeds in the fruit.

*The Spirit of God has made me; the breath
of the Almighty gives me life* (Job 33:4).

Several years ago I was invited to speak at a
church conference on the topic of discovering
your purpose in life. Before I was introduced, the
host invited a gentleman to share briefly on the
establishment of an educational institution that had
distinguished itself in that community. An unassum-
ing, middle-aged gentleman stepped forward and
began to share a story that pierced my soul. He told
of how his mother had failed in an attempt to abort
him as an unborn child, and he had ended up living
in foster homes all over the city for many years. He
emphasized how he had dreamed of providing an
environment in which young people could grow and
learn so that they would not have to suffer what he
had experienced.

He introduced to the audience the school he had
founded and established—a school that had become
one of the leading academic institutions for high
school students in that city.

Imagine if his mother had been successful. She
would have killed a school. Despite his past and his
less-than-ideal heritage, this dreamer rose above his
circumstances and maximized his potential, which is
now benefiting generations to come.

Now finish the work, so that your eager willingness to do it may be matched by your completion of it, according to your means (2 Corinthians 8:11).

The prophet Elijah also exemplifies the importance of living to the fullest and refusing to settle for present circumstances. As recorded in the Book of First Kings, Elijah confronted the prophets of baal and challenged them to a contest to prove whether baal or Jehovah was the true God. After much prayer and dancing by the prophets of baal, they had no results. Then Elijah called on the Lord God, and fire fell and consumed the sacrifice. Afterward, he commanded the people to seize the prophets of baal, and all were destroyed. When Queen Jezebel, a worshiper of baal, heard this news, she sent a message to Elijah, threatening his life. (See 1 Kings 18:16–19:4.)

After all Elijah's great accomplishments and achievements, this distinguished prophet had a death wish with suicidal tendencies. God was not persuaded. He intervened and showed Elijah that he had much more to accomplish before his full potential and purpose would be maximized.

Suppose Elijah had died when he wanted to quit. If so, his successor, Elisha, who performed twice as many miracles as Elijah, would not have discovered his purpose and fulfilled his potential.

So the next generation would know them, even the children yet to be born, and they in turn would tell their children (Psalm 78:6).

I wonder how many thousands, perhaps millions, of people will be poorer because they cannot benefit from the awesome wealth of the treasure of your potential: the books you have neglected to write, the songs you have yet to compose, or the inventions you continue to postpone. Perhaps there are millions who need the ministry or business you have yet to establish. You must maximize your life for the sake of the future. The next generation needs your potential.

What a sense of destiny, purpose, and accomplishment is contained in the Scriptures. There is no hint of regret or remorse, only confidence and personal satisfaction.

Millions of the world's population, both now and in generations passed, have poured out some of their potential, accomplished some of their dreams, and achieved some of their goals. Still, because they have refused to maximize their lives, their cup holds a portion of their purpose, stagnating into depression, regret, and death.

I admonish you, decide today to act on the rest of your sleeping dreams. Commit yourself to the goal of dying empty.

His children will be mighty in the land; the generation of the upright will be blessed (Psalm 112:2).

First discover what you were born to be, then do it. Fulfill your own personal purpose for the glory of God. *Your obedience to God's will and purpose for your life is a personal decision, but not a private one.* God has designed the universe in such a way that the purposes of all human beings are interdependent; your purpose affects millions. Maximizing your potential is, therefore, necessary and critical. Your sphere of influence is much greater than your private world.

Suppose Mary had aborted Jesus, or Andrew had failed to introduce Peter to Jesus. What if Abraham had not left the Land of Ur, or Joseph had refused to go to Egypt? Or let's assume that Ananias had not prayed for Saul who became Paul, or that the little boy had refused to give Jesus his lunch. How different the biblical record might read! These examples show that although our obedience is always a personal decision, it is never a private matter.

Don't rob the next generation of your contribution to the destiny of mankind. Maximize yourself for God's glory.

You have been set free from sin and have become slaves to righteousness (Romans 6:18).

The cry, "We want to be free!" has swept our world in remarkable and frightening ways within the past two decades. Particularly in Eastern Europe, the desire for freedom brought sweeping revolutions, toppling governments and power structures that have repressed and oppressed many peoples. This same yearning for freedom prompts pregnant women to abort their babies, children to take their parents to court, and students to seek greater control over the measures of discipline used in their schools.

Freedom! It sounds so good. Everybody wants freedom. Ethnic groups, social groups, religious groups. Children, youth, adults. It should not surprise us, then, that many common phrases express this craving for freedom: freedom of the press, freedom of choice, freedom of religion, freedom of speech. All reveal the universal longing to be unencumbered by the dictates and the decisions of others.

Is this truly possible? Can we be entirely free? No, I don't think so. Nothing is free. Although advertising tries to convince us that we are getting something for nothing—buy one, get one free—we are still paying for the product the advertiser claims is free. We cannot get something for nothing.

All forms of freedom carry a responsibility with them.

But now that you have been set free from sin and have become slaves to God, the benefit you reap leads to holiness, and the result is eternal life (Romans 6:22).

When we seek freedom without responsibility, that freedom will bring negative consequences.

When the serpent convinced Adam and Eve to eat from the one tree, God put them out of the Garden and they lost the freedom to eat from the Garden's other trees. *The first penalty of freedom without responsibility is **the loss of existing freedoms.***

***Slavery** is a second consequence of freedom without responsibility.* When the man and the woman disobeyed God and ate from the tree of the knowledge of good and evil, they became slaves to evil. They could no longer see and do what God requires. This loss of the ability to see and do what is right is always a result of choosing to place oneself above the law.

*The third consequence of freedom without responsibility is **death**.* The teenager who indulges in late hours will eventually see the death of his parents' trust. Likewise, the politician who neglects to fulfill his promises will suffer the death of his dream for advancement and recognition.

All who sin apart from the law will also perish apart from the law, and all who sin under the law will be judged by the law (Romans 2:12).

———•———

A *law* regulates and governs the behavior of someone or something.

A *command* expresses the will of the authority based upon the established rules and regulations that govern the group. Thus, a *commandment* specifies behavior relative to a law.

A *demand* assumes that the requester has the right to make the request, and it specifies behavior in a specific instance or circumstance.

As the head of the home, the father may establish the law that the privacy of each individual is ensured. This is a given within the structure of the family. Then he may issue the command that all members of the family should knock on a closed bedroom door and wait for the bidding "come in" before entering that room. This is his mandate or commandment relative to the principle of ensuring the privacy of each individual.

God's laws, commands, and demands are His means of helping you fulfill your potential.

But I gave them this command: Obey Me, and I will be your God and you will be My people. Walk in all the ways I command you, that it may go well with you (Jeremiah 7:23).

———————•——•———————

God has established many laws that influence our lives. Some of these govern the physical world in which we live; others control our relationships within the human family and with God Himself. For example, God has established marriage as the structure in which sexual relationships should be enjoyed and children should be raised. That is His law. *"You shall not commit adultery"* (Exod. 20:14) is one of His commandments built on that law.

God's demands are always based on His laws and commandments. He is not capricious, nor is He out to destroy our pleasure. *He knows that we cannot fulfill our potential outside His laws*, so He gives us commandments relative to those laws and He makes demands on us that apply His commandments to our situation. The law of love is a good example of this principle.

Yet, you control the impact of God's laws on your life because the decision to obey or disobey God's commandments and demands is wholly yours. In this manner, *you control your destiny.*

This is love for God: to obey His commands. And His commands are not burdensome (1 John 5:3).

If something sounds too good to be true, it probably is. Pro-choice groups may persuade us that we are free to abort our babies, but they do not warn us of the severe depression and never-ending sense of loss that plague many women following an abortion. Cigarette ads may portray healthy, laughing men and women puffing away on the particular brand that tastes best and gives the most satisfying high, but they do not show the hospital rooms, cancer treatment centers, and doctors' offices filled with smokers suffering from lung cancer and emphysema.

The Scriptures are clear that God's laws are good. Through *thou shalt nots* God delineates the limits within which you can live a healthy, happy, productive life. They are His means of helping you. He does not intend to unnecessarily harm, restrict, or bind you.

God created you to fulfill your potential, but you must accept the principles and laws that govern it. That's the bottom line.

We know that the law is good if one uses it properly (1 Timothy 1:8).

The limitless ability God has given us to do all we can think, to accomplish all we can imagine, to fulfill every aspiration we entertain cannot survive unless we obey God's laws and live within His limitations. Let us examine some of the misconceptions that surround the concept of law.

Misconception #1—Laws Restrict Us

All parents have heard the complaint, "You just don't want me to have any fun," when they put a restriction upon their children's activities. Very often we transfer this same attitude into our relationship with God. We see God's thou shalt nots as His means of taking the fun out of life.

Misconception #2—Laws Inhibit Us

The misconception that law inhibits or restrains us also distorts our understanding of the purpose of law. This perception is readily evident in the attitude of the employee who feels that the obligation to punch a time clock cramps her preferred style of arriving at work five or ten minutes after the designated starting time and making up that time at the end of the day.

But showing love to a thousand generations of those who love Me and keep My commandments (Deuteronomy 5:10).

Misconception #3—Laws Bind Us

Some laws appear to bind us and we, therefore, find them to be irritating. Traffic laws are good examples of these laws. One day as I rode in the car with my son, I tried to beat a yellow light because I was a little late. As the light changed, my son said, "Daddy, the light is changing." Just as I pressed the accelerator to make the light, he spoke again, "Daddy, you've got to stop," and then, "Thou goest too fast, O Dad." The law concerning red lights was particularly binding to me that day.

Misconception #4—Laws Rob Us

The belief that laws prevent us from receiving the best things of life is also a false understanding of the nature of law. A young Christian girl who wants to marry a nice-looking, well-behaved guy who isn't saved thinks God is unfair when He says not to be yoked with unbelievers (see 2 Cor. 6:14).

All these misconceptions convince us that laws and regulations are encumbrances and burdens that prevent us from enjoying life to the fullest. In truth, laws are provided for our benefit.

*He who scorns instruction will pay for it,
but he who respects a command is rewarded* (Proverbs 13:13).

It is reported that the late newspaper counselor,
Ann Landers, received an average of 10,000 letters each month. Nearly all these letters were from
people who were burdened with problems. When
Landers was asked if one type of problem was pre-
dominant in these letters, she replied that *fear* was
the one problem above all others. People fear losing
their health and their loved ones. Many potentially
great men and women are afraid of life itself. They
never attempt their dreams because they fear failure.
Others fail to strive for their aspirations because they
fear success and the responsibility and accountabili-
ty that comes with any measure of success.

We do not need to fear if we obey God's laws.
Laws are given to help us and to make life more
enjoyable. How do they accomplish their purpose?
What reliable benefits do they offer?

First, *laws protect us*. They alert us to possible
danger. The child who lives with no rules and
restrictions is much more likely to get hurt or to end
up in trouble than the child who lives within a structure of parental guidance.

Great peace have they who love Your law, and nothing can make them stumble (Psalm 119:165).

Perhaps it is the inherent ability to explore the impossible for the possibilities that Jesus Christ, the most maximized Man who ever lived, referred to when He stated, *"...unless you change and become like little children, you will never enter the kingdom of heaven"* (Matt. 18:3).

Laws give us assistance to explore the possibilities. Can you imagine the confusion if everyone addressed their letters however they wished? Some people might put the address of the sender in the upper left corner, but others might put the address of the recipient there. Or one community might have the tradition of putting the stamp on the back of the envelope, while every other community places it on the front. Postal regulations aid the efficient handling of mail so letters go to the sender's intended recipient.

Instead of restraining us, laws provide assistance so we can accomplish what we intend.

Let the peace of Christ rule in your hearts, since as members of one body you were called to peace. And be thankful (Colossians 3:15).

*L*aws also allow us to express ourselves complete-ly within the context of community. Consider what would happen if you bought a house in a nice neighborhood to raise your children in a safe, non-violent environment only to have your neighbor open an adults-only bookstore. The traffic on your formerly quiet street now quadruples and your children are exposed to unhealthy materials as people come from the shop leafing through pornographic literature.

One night a patron is shot in front of your house by his wife, who is enraged by his attitudes and his actions toward her. Suddenly, your nice neighborhood is no longer safe. Civil laws help to control what is and is not permitted within a community so that all may enjoy the environment they desire.

Laws allow each person to enjoy his individual preferences so long as he does not infringe on the freedom of others to do the same.

*...live by the Spirit, and you will not grati-
fy the desires of the sinful nature. For the
sinful nature desires what is contrary to the
Spirit...But if you are led by the Spirit, you
are not under law* (Galatians 5:16-18).

*L*aws help us to do and be our best. The very laws
that restrict negative behavior also encourage
and uphold positive attitudes and actions. The rule
that makes the entire class responsible for monitor-
ing cheating and gives a failing grade to anyone who
copies from another student's paper also encourages
excellence because it exerts peer pressure for honesty. Thus, the law both sets consequences for negative behavior and rewards those who work hard and
do their best.

The Bible clearly shows that laws do not restrict
positive thoughts and behavior:

*The acts of the sinful nature are obvious:
sexual immorality, impurity and debauch-
ery; idolatry and witchcraft; hatred, dis-
cord, jealousy, fits of rage, selfish ambition,
dissensions, factions and envy; drunken-
ness, orgies, and the like. I warn you...that
those who live like this will not inherit the
kingdom of God. But the fruit of the Spirit
is love, joy, peace, patience, kindness,
goodness, faithfulness, gentleness and self-
control. Against such things there is no law*
(Galatians 5:19-23).

And whatever you do, whether in word or deed, do it all in the name of the Lord Jesus, giving thanks to God the Father through Him (Colossians 3:17).

*L*aw allows us to function within God's general design for human life, and the plans and purposes He sets for our individual lives.

The blessing of the Lord brings wealth, and He adds no trouble to it (Proverbs 10:22).

Achieving purpose with God's blessing never brings sorrow. Those, however, who try to fulfill their potential outside His purposes often experience multiplied sorrow. A businessman, for example, who builds his business without God's guidance and direction may attain the same wealth as a man who submitted his dreams and plans to God's will, but his position outside God's plan does not provide the freedom from worry that the other businessman enjoys.

When the Lord blesses a person with prosperity, He both protects what He has given and He serves as a resource to the recipient. Humans need spiritual resources as surely as we need physical and material assets.

Potential without law is dangerous. Law is His safeguard to keep us from self-destructing.

Everyone who sins breaks the law; in fact,
sin is lawlessness (1 John 3:4).

Many people throughout history have harmed themselves and others because they tried to fulfill their potential outside God's specifications. Adolf Hitler, for example, was a gifted leader. Using his leadership skills, he came up through the ranks of government until he was legally elected the chancellor of Germany. Once he achieved that position, something went wrong. He violated the rules of leadership.

Hitler violated that law and made himself a dictator. Instead of using his power to serve and bless the country he ruled, he placed himself above the law and forced people to do his bidding. Hitler also broke the laws of human dignity and equality because he created and enforced policies that treated people who were not of Aryan descent as subhumans and half-humans who were created to serve the perfect race. Many Jews and other non-Aryan peoples were victims of Hitler's beliefs and policies.

Potential is always given to bless, never to harm. If your potential is hurting someone or something, you'd better look carefully at your attitudes and actions.

As for you, you were dead in your transgressions and sins (Ephesians 2:1).

———•———

Let's say, for example, that you are a young executive in a local bank. You have worked at the bank for five years, developing a good working knowledge of the banking industry and building a solid reputation for honesty and integrity. Your goal is to become the manager of the main branch.

However, your spouse constantly complains that you don't earn enough, until one day, in desperation, you take $2,000 from the bank safe and give it to your spouse. Several things happen when you do this. First, you lose the protection of your good reputation. Until now, people have trusted not only your integrity but also the soundness of your decisions. Second, you forfeit the opportunity to rise to the position of branch manager. Third, you interrupt your career because not only the bank you worked for but other employers as well cannot trust you. This one act of disregarding the commandment *"You shall not steal"* (Exod. 20:15) destroys your potential to become a competent, respected banker.

You must abide by God's specifications to enjoy the totality of who you are.

You were taught, with regard to your former way of life, to put off your old self... and to but on the new self, created to be like God in true righteousness and holiness (Ephesians 4:22,24).

———•———

A hush fell over the room as a petite, neatly groomed woman stepped to the podium in the prison room. Her first words startled them. "I am one of you. I lived here for five years. I came here at the age of 20, leaving behind my husband and my young daughter. Although it has been many years since my release, I still remember the intense loneliness and the consuming despair that filled my first days here. I can also hear in my mind the click of the gate behind me. I doubt those thoughts and feelings will ever leave me."

"I am here today because something very important happened to me here. I met the Lord Jesus Christ, accepted His forgiveness for my past, and entrusted my future to His keeping. My life is very different because of Him. Through His love and mercy, and the support and encouragement of many brothers and sisters in Christ, I have finally forgiven myself for the wrongs that brought me here. Today I am free because He freed me, and I bring to you the opportunity to find this freedom and forgiveness."

The Lord is compassionate and gracious, slow to anger abounding in love....He removed our transgressions from us (Psalm 103:8,12).

Self-forgiveness is often difficult. God forgives and forgets our sin as soon as we confess it. We, on the other hand, often hold ourselves accountable for our wrongs for a long time. Indeed, many who have accepted Jesus Christ as their Savior still think and act as though their sins are not forgiven.

Remember, God's promises are true and His power surpasses all other powers. *If God says your sins are forgiven, they are forgiven. You are freed forever from their penalty and their power over you. No one, including satan, has the authority or the right to change or dispute His decision.*

The failure to forgive ourselves places us at risk for future sin. Refuse, then, to allow self-condemnation to steal your potential in Christ. If you have confessed your sin, you are forgiven and God remembers it no more. Forgive yourself and move on. If you would love others and share your potential with them, you must first love and forgive yourself. This is an important step in the journey of recovering your potential.

Create in me a pure heart, O God, and renew a steadfast spirit within me.... Restore to me the joy of Your salvation and grant me a willing spirit, to sustain me (Psalm 51:10,12).

A ll of us have things in our pasts of which we are ashamed. While self-forgiveness takes away the sting of those confessed sins, it does not remove from our minds the memory of those wrongs. We must learn to live with our memories and allow them to be a positive force in our lives.

King David, after his sin with Bathsheba, most certainly was haunted by his wrong (see 2 Sam. 11:1–12:25). Overwhelmed by the enormity of his sin, he could have forfeited his potential to serve God as the king of God's people. Instead, David confessed his sin (see 2 Sam. 12:13 and Ps. 51) and petitioned God. Today David is remembered as a man after God's heart and the greatest king in the history of God's people.

This same restorative power of God can move you beyond the negative opinions, poor judgments, unhealthy relationships, detrimental environments, and adverse circumstances of your past. No sin is too great for God to forgive. No memory is too deep for Him to heal. No problem is beyond His blessing and power.

*I press on toward the goal to win the prize
for which God has called me heavenward
in Christ Jesus* (Philippians 3:14).

*T*he greatest threat to being all you could be is
satisfaction with who you are. What you could
do is always endangered by what you have done.
There are millions of individuals who have buried
their latent talents, gifts, and abilities in the cemetery of their last accomplishment. They have settled
for less than their best. I believe that the enemy of
best is *good*, and the strength of *good* is the *norm*.
The power of the norm is the curse of our society. It
seems like the world is designed to make "the norm"
comfortable and "the average" respectable. What a
tragedy!

A quick glance at history reveals that the individuals who impacted their generations and affected
the world most dramatically were individuals who,
because of a circumstance, pressure, or decision,
challenged the tide of convention, stretched the
boundaries of tradition, and violated the expectations of the norm. *Few great things have ever been
done within the confines of the accepted norm.*

And the ransomed of the Lord will return. They will enter Zion with singing; everlasting joy will crown their heads. Gladness and joy will overtake them, and sorrow and sighing will flee away (Isaiah 35:10).

I learned a lesson that would become a major pillar in my life. I ignored the manufacturer's manual that came with a newly purchased video player/recorder. Because I refused to read and follow the instructions contained therein, I was unable to utilize, maximize, and fully appreciate the full potential of the product. I was settling for less than full capacity. I was a victim of living according to the standards and observations of others. This limitation of performance can also be extended to those who read the manufacturer's manual but refuse to use the functions inherent in the construction of the product. Therefore, they never experience the full potential of the machine.

In reality, this experience perfectly describes the lives of most of the nearly 6 billion people on planet Earth. Many live on only four functions: play, stop, pause, and rewind. Day after day they go to jobs they hate, stop to rest in homes they despise, pause long enough to vent their frustration, and then play the games people play pretending to be happy.

Whatever your hand finds to do, do it with all your might, for in the grave, where you are going, there is neither working nor planning nor knowledge nor wisdom (Ecclesiastes 9:10).

———◆———

I am convinced that our Creator never intended for us to be *normal*—that is, to get lost in the crowd of "the norm." This is evidenced by the fact that among the 5.8 billion people on this planet, no two individuals are alike; their fingerprints, genetic code, and chromosome combinations are all distinct and unique. In reality, God created all people to be originals, but we continue to become copies of others. Too often we are so preoccupied with trying to fit in, that we never stand out.

You were designed to be distinctive, special, irreplaceable, and unique, so refuse to be "normal"! Go beyond average! Do not strive to be accepted, rather strive to be yourself. Shun the minimum; pursue the maximum. Utilize all your functions—maximize yourself!

Live life with all your might; give it all you have. Do it until there is nothing left to do because you have become all you were created to be, done all you were designed to do, and given all you were sent to give. Be satisfied with nothing less than your best.

Yet to all who received Him, to those who believed in His name, He gave the right to become children of God—children born not of natural descent, nor of human decision or a husband's will, but born of God (John 1:12-13).

*A*n important step to recovering our potential is to redeem the time that is left to us. We cannot undo what is past, but we can make the necessary changes in our lives to permit the wise use of the remainder of our days.

Time is God's gift for accomplishing our purpose and fulfilling our potential. It begins the day we are born and ends when we die. The length of our physical life matches the days required to fulfill our purpose because God planned for the maturing of our lives within the total days He has allotted to us. Therefore, *we have sufficient time to maximize our potential.* The question is, will we waste or use wisely the days God has assigned to our lives?

Consciously refuse to allow procrastination, discouragement, and the other enemies of your potential to induce you to waste even one day of your life.

Fear of man will prove to be a snare [trap of restriction], but whoever trusts in the Lord [in the assessment of his Creator] *is kept safe* (Proverbs 29:25).

Most of our social and cultural environment works against our dreams and minimizes the magnitude and scope of the vision in our hearts. We are trained mentally and spiritually to fear our dreams and doubt our destiny. We are discouraged into believing that our passion for greatness is abnormal and our aspirations are suspect. The result of this human "counter-development" process is that the majority of the earth's population lives under the spell and debilitating power of the specter called "fear."

Fear is the source of 90 percent of the lack of progress and personal development in the lives of millions of gifted, talented, and resourceful individuals. Many experts in the field of human behavior have stated that the fear of failure and the fear of success are the two most powerful and most prevalent fears experienced by the human family.

What a sad and depressing way to live. I challenge you to step away from the crowd of those who maintain, and join the few who are committed to attaining their full potential by endeavoring to maximize their abilities.

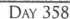
Nathan replied to David, "Whatever you have in mind, do it, for God is with you" (1 Chronicles 17:2).

A few years ago I was invited to the beautiful nation of Brazil to address a leadership conference. During my stay there, my host took me to visit a little town made famous by a sculptor who had lost both hands to the disease of leprosy. As a young man stricken with this horrible disease, he would sit for many hours and watch his father work in his wood carving shop. One day the young man decided to train himself to carve and sculpt wood with his feet and the parts of his arms he had not lost to the leprosy.

The resilient spirit of this young man released his untapped potential, and his work gave evidence that trapped within this cripple was one of the greatest artists the world has ever known. I stood in amazement and disbelief as I viewed some of his magnificent works of wood, installed in the most beautiful churches in that city. We also visited his rendition of the major Old Testament prophets, 12 life-sized carvings that are displayed as one of Brazil's most admired national treasures.

There is no limit to our potential except that which is self-imposed.

Jesus looked at them and said, "With man this is impossible, but not with God; all things are possible with God" (Mark 10:27).

Jesus Christ, the specimen of humanity who best demonstrated the unlimited nature of the potential in humankind, said, *"Everything is possible for him who believes"* (Mark 9:23b). What daring spirit this statement ignites. It makes us question our own limitations and disagree with our fears.

The Master Creator and Designer established His purpose for each item in creation and built into each the ability or potential to perform and fulfill that purpose or assignment.

Your life is a result of a purpose in the mind of God that requires your existence. You were created because *there is something God wants done that demands your presence on this planet.* You were designed and dispatched for destiny. This destiny and purpose is also the key to your ability. You were created with the inherent abilities, talents, gifts, and inclinations to fulfill this purpose. Just as a bird is designed to fly, a fish to swim, and an apple tree to bear fruit, even so you possess the potential to be all you were born to be. Your life has the potential to fulfill your purpose.

"My food," said Jesus, *"is to do the will of Him who sent Me and to finish His work* (John 4:34).

———✦———

You, and every other individual, possess the responsibility for this awesome treasure buried within, because this treasure within you can be fully released only if you are willing to believe and accept God's dream for your life. If you are willing to submit to His will and purpose for your destiny and to cooperate with His specifications, nothing will be impossible for you.

Determine not to be satisfied with anything less than the full accomplishment of your dream. Surrender to the demands that maximize your potential so that none of your assignment is left undone when you leave this planet. The responsibility to use what God has stored within you is yours alone.

Many individuals are aware of their ability and potential, but they have become frustrated and disillusioned by either their past failures or the negative influence of others. They have chosen to limit or withhold the wonderful gift the Creator has invested in them. Therefore, I strongly urge you to rise up from your temporary fears, shake yourself, and step out once again on the road to being and becoming your true self.

And do this, understanding the present time. The hour has come for you to wake up from your slumber, because our salvation is nearer now than when we first believed (Romans 13:11).

The release and maximization of something's potential is dependent on an environment that is conducive to its development and release. For instance, despite the potential of a seed to produce a tree after its kind and to bring forth fruit in abundance, this great potential can be minimized, restrained, or immobilized by an improper environmental condition. If the seed is placed on a baked clay tile or a stone, or in a polluted substance or toxic elements, its great potential will be restricted and never fully maximized.

This limitation of potential not only robs the seed of the right to fulfill its true potential but it also robs birds of food and of branches for their nests, and deprives people of wood for building houses, of fruit for food, and of fuel for heat and cooking. Therefore, any attempt to restrict, abuse, misuse, oppress, or repress the potential of any living thing has a direct effect on the purpose and will of God.

Wisdom is a shelter as money is a shelter,
but the advantage of knowledge is this: that
wisdom preserves the life of its possessor
(Ecclesiastes 7:12).

The magnitude and depth of human potential on earth has yet to be tapped. Millions are born, live, and die never discovering or exposing the awesome potential that resides within them. This tragic state of affairs, which is a global phenomenon, is the result of man's succumbing to life governed by his own devices. The major source of this tragedy is ignorance.

As mentioned previously, the most powerful enemy of mankind is not sin or satan, but the death-dealing, life-stealing force called ignorance. The Old Testament prophet Hosea recognized ignorance as the primary source of personal, social, and national destruction. When relaying God's explanation for moral and social decay among the nations, he wrote, *"My people are destroyed from lack of knowledge"* (Hos. 4:6a). The implication is that destruction in any area of our lives, whether personally or nationally, is related to a lack of knowledge.

The ignorance of humans about humans is the ultimate cause of all our problems. The truth about us is found in God's Word.

"For if you remain silent at this time, relief and deliverance for the Jews will arise from another place, but you and your father's family will perish. And who knows but that you have come to royal position for such a time as this?" (Esther 4:14)

We have all been created to serve the purposes of God as partners in dominion over creation, for the purpose of manifesting God's nature. God created each of us with the spirit of leadership and the aspiration to determine our own destiny. This sacred spirit must be respected, protected, and properly related to God, the Creator, or its power will be turned toward others to oppress us.

This has been the plight of all Third World people. They have fallen victim to the ignorance of men concerning the equality and purpose for humankind.

The millions of Third World people in Europe, Asia, Africa, and the Americas, including those who are quietly buried within the walls of the industrial states, must now determine to loose themselves from the mental shackles of the oppressor; to honor the dignity, value, and worth of their brothers; and to provide an environment within which the corporate will and energy of the people may be developed.

But now, O Lord, Thou art our Father; we are the clay, and Thou our potter; and we all are the work of Thy hand (Isaiah 64:8 KJV).

Discovering and developing your potential is your blessing from God. Let's review some of the important principles and keys that will help you become the person God intended:

1. God gave you an eternal spirit with eternal potential.
2. Sin has robbed you of that potential because you are born spiritually dead.
3. God redeemed your eternal potential through the death of Jesus.
4. You were designed to live by faith.
5. Faith is believing, seeing, releasing, and receiving.

You have been created to:

1. Express God's image.
2. Enjoy fellowship with God.
3. Dominate the earth.
4. Bear fruit.
5. Reproduce yourself.

*He also says, "In the beginning, O Lord,
You laid the foundations of the earth, and
the heavens are the work of Your hands"*
(Hebrews 1:10).

———◆———

Jesus is our ultimate model of Someone who discovered, developed, and died empty of His potential. He reached the goal His heavenly Father set for Him. He redeemed us—He set us free.

Remember these important concepts as you rejoice in His loving kindness:

1. Our potential is to be poured out for the sake of the Kingdom of God.
2. Mediocrity is living below our known, true potential.
3. Success is a journey of discovery and adventure as you explore your God-given potential.
4. What you have done does not equal the sum of what you can do.
5. God is your Source.
6. Work is God's blessing to challenge and expose your potential.
7. Satan is your enemy—your dreams, plans, and ideas are his targets.
8. Guard and protect your potential.
9. Cultivate and feed your potential.
10. Share your potential.

Will you take the step today to fulfill your potential—your destiny? I pray so.

REFLECTIONS

_____

_____

_____

_____

_____

_____

_____

_____

_____

_____

_____

_____

_____

_____

_____

_____

_____

_____

_____

_____

_____

_____

_____

_____

REFLECTIONS

REFLECTIONS

REFLECTIONS

REFLECTIONS

REFLECTIONS

REFLECTIONS

REFLECTIONS

REFLECTIONS

_____
_____
_____
_____
_____
_____
_____
_____
_____
_____
_____
_____
_____
_____
_____
_____
_____
_____
_____
_____
_____
_____
_____
_____
_____
_____